I AM YOUR
BROTHER JOSEPH

I AM YOUR BROTHER JOSEPH

✠

Cardinal Bernardin of Chicago

Tim Unsworth

A Crossroad Book
The Crossroad Publishing Company
New York

1997

The Crossroad Publishing Company
370 Lexington Avenue, New York, NY 10017

Printed in the United States of America

Library of Congress Catalog Card Number: 96-72245
ISBN 0-8245-1667-2

To Jean
blessed among women

Now as always, Christ will be magnified in my body, whether by life or by death. For to me life is Christ, and death is gain. If I go on living in the flesh, that means fruitful labor for me. And I do not know which I shall choose. I am caught between the two. I long to depart this life and be with Christ, for that is far better. Yet that I remain in the flesh is more necessary for your benefit. . . . Only conduct yourselves in a way worthy of the gospel of Christ, so that, whether I come to see you or am absent . . . you are standing firm in one spirit, with one mind struggling together for the faith of the gospel.

—Philippians 1

I am [afraid of death] every time I let myself be seduced by the noisy voices of my world telling me that my 'little life' is all I have and advising me to cling to it with all my might. But when I let these voices move to the background of my life and listen to that small soft voice calling me the Beloved, I know there is nothing to fear and that dying is the greatest act of love, the act that leads me into the eternal embrace of my God whose love is everlasting.

—Henri J. M. Nouwen
Life of the Beloved, 1992

Contents

Preface

A T A MEMORIAL LITURGY for the media held a few days after his funeral at Chicago's Quigley High School Seminary, just a few blocks from his office, Joseph Louis Bernardin was recalled as a man who loved the media. He never viewed it as a threat or as a group of suppliants grateful for decrees pushed under their doors. He used it often to bring Sandburg's "City of Big Shoulders" to its knees, especially during the weeks that preceded and followed his funeral. While other church leaders often railed at the media much as politicians do routinely, Bernardin treated it as a friend — a conduit between his cathedral throne and the kitchen chairs of his faithful.

His close friend Msgr. Kenneth Velo, who had served as his executive assistant for over a decade, recalled that Cardinal Bernardin began each day with prayer, a light breakfast, and at least three major newspapers. At his office, his FYI folders were often filled with "need to know" clippings. If he couldn't watch the noon news, he somehow managed to learn from others if there was any church-related news. In the early evening he caught the television news and, if he had an evening appointment, he would try to return home in time to absorb more. If he was late for the 10:00 p.m. broadcast, he would ask one of his priest companions. His appetite for news was insatiable.

Occasionally, some overprotective staff would withhold news from him, particularly news appearing in some ultra-conservative Catholic papers which took an almost perverse delight in hammering him. It was hard to blame his staff. Strong criticism hurt

11

him, particularly if it was inaccurate or personal. It hurt even more that many of his fellow prelates would not defend him, often in the face of libelous criticism. From time to time, he would speak of his "enemies." It took me years to realize that he was referring — at least occasionally — to his brother bishops.

I considered him a friend and generally wrote sentiments that others occasionally saw as pandering. Yet, I stung him a few times, even causing anger. He once responded in print, terming my observations "sociological in nature and that only by way of observation." (I wanted to reply, informing him that my figures came from his own Office of Planning. But, somehow, the cardinal would never let anyone get that mad at him. He disarmed even while he disagreed. Besides, his tart letter sounded as if it were written by a nervous staffer. Bernardin's word linkages just weren't there.)

In a way he was too sensitive. Yet, the alternative would simply not have been him.

"He would drive us nuts with his corrections and clarifications," Sister M. Brian Costello, R.S.M., his chief of staff, recalled affectionately. His research theologian, Fr. Michael Place, called it "procedural impeccability." He was constantly attempting to find an angle of repose between administrative and philosophical consistency and the need to rise above principle. He was a man who viewed life through a telescope, not in a rear-view mirror. He did virtually all of his work with the media looking over his shoulder. He viewed it as an instrument of communication.

A book such as this is a natural extension of the mammoth publicity his dying and death caused. I wanted to write it with him, in an "as-told-to" fashion. We talked about it over dinner and exchanged pleasant letters about my written proposal. But for a lot of reasons he demurred. I wanted to include background to his seamless garment metaphor; he felt that the consistent ethic of life theology was not yet fully developed. I wanted to have him write about the charges of sexual abuse that had been brought against him; he likely felt that it was a subject only he could write intimately about. I wanted him to provide others with his reflections on dying. He ended up doing this himself in a small, moving book, *The Gift of Peace* published in early 1997 (Loyola University Press).

We were good friends, but I was not alone in this friendship. His good friend of over thirty years Eugene Kennedy had already written two books about him and would update his first biography following his death. He even considered as his biographer the late Henri Nouwen, a priest who had helped him face death, but Nouwen himself died just a few months before the cardinal.

He liked me. My often flip style amused him. But he was much too cautious a man to entrust his complex life to my sentences. In an earlier book, *Last Priests in America* (Crossroad, 1991), I had devoted the longest of its forty-two chapters to him. Even before the interview, we had agreed that he could review the initial draft. He didn't tell me to change a word, but he made enough "corrections" even in his direct quotations to make me regret that I had agreed. In his generally favorable review in the *Washington Post*, Colman McCarthy described the Bernardin chapter as "the longest and dullest." It would have sparkled if the cardinal had not been so careful.

This book does not pretend to be a definitive biography of Cardinal Joseph Bernardin. Clearly, such a history needs to be done. He deserves something akin to John Tracy Ellis's monumental life of Cardinal James Gibbons of Baltimore. Chances are, a church historian will attempt the task.

I Am Your Brother Joseph: Cardinal Bernardin of Chicago is an anecdotal biography of the best-known and best-loved bishop in America. It is an informal portrait, not a formal canvas. It is hardly an objective treatment. I considered him one of the most pastorally sensitive and politically shrewd people I have ever known. He was a humble man at a level within the church where one generally finds only inflated ego. But he had a healthy ego that always reminded him of who and what he was.

Bernardin understood the difference between leadership and authority. He was a shepherd who would could lead without building fences. After fourteen years of observing him, it is almost impossible to be objective about him. I feel about him as Elisha did about the prophet Elijah: "Please," Elisha prayed, "let me inherit a double share of your spirit" (2 Kings 2:9).

It is my hope that readers of this book will get a double share of the spirit of the man whose motto was "As Those Who Serve."

I AM YOUR
BROTHER JOSEPH

"I am your brother Joseph. . . .
God sent me before you to preserve life."

—Gen. 45:4–5

ONE

Death as a Friend

M Y FIRST CALL came at 10:30 a.m. on August 30, 1996. "What's happening?" asked Mary Ann Ahern, a TV reporter for NBC News in Chicago.

Although I had followed Cardinal Joseph Bernardin's comings and goings since he was appointed archbishop of Chicago in July 1982, I was still outside the clerical and media loop that surrounded America's best-known bishop. As a freelance writer, I wasn't an accredited reporter assigned to the Archdiocesan Pastoral Center. I wasn't on their list of people to call when an announcement was to be made. However, I generally got wind of any breaking news, and, although the chancery office has fairly tight security and a sign-in ritual for all media, observers like myself were never turned away. The system is like the church itself: strict rules but not necessarily strict observance.

The security force, composed largely of retired Chicago police officers, is as friendly as my pastor. They had watched the cardinal come and go and had come to treasure his common touch. I visited with them often, partly to avail of the chancery's bathroom — a haven for a freelance writer.

Mary Ann Ahern was curious. Cardinal Bernardin was holding his third press conference is less than six weeks, an extraordinary number even for a bishop who had pledged to keep his people fully informed about almost every move he made. There was a palpable urgency about this announcement and more than the usual pre-conference attempts at secrecy. Ahern had been told that the news was of "a deeply personal nature." She said that her caller was a bit choked up.

Ahern herself was upset. She had interviewed the cardinal often. She liked him. A devout Catholic herself, spouse of an ATF agent, and mother of three, she had more than a professional interest in news about the church. It was in her blood.

✠

Every reporter has sources within any organization. Without sources, a TV or print reporter might as well be an ad taker. The church is no exception. Indeed, it leaks like an old ark. There is something healthy about such leaks. They reflect an interest and energy within the organization. Gossip-free institutions are generally unhealthy or indifferent.

I made three calls to the Pastoral Center on Superior Street — a street name that cynical priests liked to joke about. (It is actually named for Lake Superior, the largest of the five Great Lakes.) I got nowhere. No one wanted to talk. The news had to be serious.

Notice of the press conference and its contents had already been distributed to the many offices within the building. Phone calls had already been made to the six auxiliary bishops, and a letter had been sent to the priests of the archdiocese. When I called my paper, the *National Catholic Reporter* in Kansas City, Missouri, they already had a fax regarding the conference and a strong hint as to its contents.

The cardinal had gotten his doctor's report on Wednesday afternoon. For a year following his initial surgery, he had been having regular checkups every three months. "My oncologist, Dr. Ellen Gaynor, always informed me of my condition as soon as the tests were completed," he told me on the Sunday evening following the press conference. "This time, she said nothing. I suspected something was up. So I asked her and she answered: 'We've got to talk.' I knew then that something was wrong."

Bernardin had learned that his pancreatic cancer had moved to his liver. In less than three months five large nodules had appeared there. Dr. Gaynor, who is also a Dominican Sister of Sinsinawa, Wisconsin, told him that surgery was a possibility, but that the cancer would only reoccur on the portion of the liver that had not been removed.

The cardinal spent the remainder of Wednesday and Thursday notifying his sister, Elaine Addison, in Columbia, South Carolina, and other close friends and associates. He did not tell his ninety-one-year-old mother, Maria, who lived just a few miles from him. She was a resident of a nursing home conducted by the Little Sisters of the Poor. Although very close to his mother and almost a daily visitor, he knew that she wouldn't understand. Her mind had already gone ahead of her. She knew him only sporadically, sometimes referring to him as a "patriarch."

"What do you do?" she would ask him. "I work for the church," he would answer. "That's nice, Joe," she would reply, "but they don't pay you much money."

Somehow, Maria Bernardin's failure to recognize him kept the cardinal grounded. It was a classic case of role reversal. He could speak to her as a child. "Do you love me, mother?" he would ask her. "How much do you love me?" She would respond like a child, extending her hands in an embracing gesture. ("I'm Italian, too," one of his priests, Fr. Dominic Grassi, pastor of St. Josaphat's Parish, very near the nursing home, would observe with admiration. "We like to be loved.")

On Thursday, he prepared his press statement and other letters, including communications with the Vatican and the apostolic delegate's office in Washington, D.C. The present pro-nuncio is Archbishop Agostino Cacciavillan, a professional diplomat, who is more tied to the eastern U.S. cardinals than to Chicago's archbishop. He is more likely to listen to the whispered advice of Boston's Cardinal Bernard Law or New York's Cardinal John O'Connor than to Joseph Bernardin. But the Chicago archbishop is a man driven by protocol. He respects authority even though he is measurably more liberal than the cautious and often slow-acting pro-nuncio. Besides, the apostolic delegate would be kind. After all, he had all the authority.

Turnover at the chancery is relatively high. Those who move on to other positions leave friends behind. Some leave enemies. Both friends and enemies have access to phones and fax machines. Thus, by mid-morning, hundreds knew something about the agenda of the press conference.

Within thirty minutes of Ahern's call, a publisher from Dubuque, Iowa, called to ask questions. A resigned priest in California had sent an e-mail message before noon. Once the first person knows, it's like trying to put toothpaste back in the tube.

It didn't take Mary Ann and me long to figure it out. The cardinal's cancer had returned. He was going to die.

We weren't prophets. Pancreatic cancer simply works that way.

✠

In June of 1995 Joseph Louis Bernardin was diagnosed with pancreatic cancer. He would have to undergo exploratory surgery. "I had told my doctor, Warren Furey, that I was experiencing some discomfort," Bernardin told my wife and me later. "He ordered me into Mercy Hospital at 7:30 a.m. the next morning for some tests. I told him that I had to go out of town, and he said that I shouldn't worry. He'd have me out by 9:30 a.m.

"The first tests were inconclusive," he continued. "But they pointed to a potential problem. So, I was told that they would have to put me to sleep. When I woke up, there were several doctors, bishops, and priests standing over me. I knew I was in trouble." It was classic Bernardin understatement and a sample of his low-key humor.

There were discussions as to just how to address the problem. Doctors from Mercy, Loyola and Northwestern hospitals took part.

Nothing the cardinal does is without political consequences. Had he not chosen a Catholic hospital, he ran the risk of talking out of both sides of his mouth — praising Catholic hospitals, then choosing a non-sectarian one for his own surgery. The cardinal lived constantly between a rock and a hard place.

"Not quite that way," the cardinal said later. "It was agreed that we would select the best surgeon for the job, regardless of the hospital. They wanted someone with experience in the Whipple procedure, and that man was Dr. Gerard Aranha at Loyola. He had done eight such procedures since the beginning of the year."

The cardinal entered Loyola Medical Center in Maywood, Illinois, on June 11, and was operated on the next morning. The procedure was time-consuming and tedious, lasting over seven hours. Recovery was fairly rapid — some six days — but not without its discomfort. For the normally healthy cardinal, it was an unsettling experience.

Cardinals lead relatively peaceful lives. Their shoes are shined; doors are held; meals prepared. For the most part, their daily schedules are hectic but rarely stressful. Even more than other CEOs, they are protected by layers of tradition and are often surrounded by religious and ecclesiastical stagecraft that can both attract applause and intimidate critics. "It's their flunkies who get stressed out," one faithful flunky observed. They get an enormous amount of psychic income just walking down church aisles to the music of "Ecce sacerdos magnus" (Behold! The great priest!).

Now, suddenly, Bernardin was not in control of his destiny. A tube almost as thick as a shower hose was down his throat, causing extreme discomfort. His belly throbbed with the tension of layers of stitches. Later, he confided that he begged the nurse to remove the tube. But he had to endure it for seventy-two hours.

"Could you pray at times like that?" my wife asked him. "Not at all," he said. "You can't do anything." His wonderfully honest admission was a relief to Jean, who had undergone painful surgery years before and found herself equally unable to pray.

The cardinal's progress was chronicled by dozens of reporters for the next fourteen months. He was on the front pages and the lead story on television for weeks. "How's our cardinal," a Jewish friend would ask me during a ride on our building elevator. The archbishop belonged to all.

✠

It was a simple story. A well-liked leader in a metropolis of 2.4 million Catholics was seriously ill. It was June. The major news concerned the national elections, a complicated and mud-spattered story. Bernardin's story touched people. The man whose picture was on all rectory and school walls had suddenly become real. It was a story one could get one's arms around.

Oncology specialists, including Bernardin's own, were interviewed repeatedly. Chicago and the nation were given a short course in cancer of the pancreas. His medical team became minor celebrities. It was a far cry from earlier days when, for example, Cardinal Samuel Stritch's personal physician was named a papal knight and considered part of his episcopal family. The physician and his wife often traveled with Stritch to Rome. Indeed, he is said to have borrowed his physician's scalpel to secrete into a papal conclave so that he could cut his morning grapefruit. It stands as a small example of two extraordinarily different episcopal styles that Stritch's medical records remain sealed at the archdiocesan archives, although he died in 1958.

Reporters needed only to consult their fact-filled almanacs and their Rolodex files to come up with the names of physicians willing to provide background information. If pancreatic cancer is discovered in its early stages, the sources said, surgical removal of the malignant tissues may cure it. Anticancer drugs and radiation therapy may also be used. But pancreatic cancer sends few signals. All too often, it slips by even the most thorough checkups.

The statistics from the American Cancer Society reported that some twenty-seven thousand people had been diagnosed with pancreatic cancer in 1995. Eighty percent had died within twelve months. Other sources said that only 20 percent of pancreatic cancer cases had survived more than two to five years — and these were generous estimates. The media had difficulty locating even one local patient who had survived more than five years. One poor soul was pictured on the evening news, looking like Lazarus.

The surgery was followed by the usual chemotherapy and radiation treatment. The cardinal continued to look a bit wan but the treatments had spared his hair — "What little there is of it," he would say.

Within a month following the surgery, he played host to a previously scheduled picnic on the lawn of his mansion for some seven hundred young adults. They were part of a "Theology on Tap" group under the direction of Fr. John Cusick, director of the Young Adult Ministry of the archdiocese.

Later that evening, he came to our home for dinner. He was moved by the picnic experience, but mostly by three young women who had introduced themselves to him and told him of the cancer that had swept their bodies. "I never felt more like a priest," he would say again and again.

✠

The operation changed him. The priest within him moved much closer to the surface. Later, he wrote a pastoral letter on health care that was published in *America* magazine. In it he stated that during his convalescence, he "found the nights to be especially long....I sometimes found myself weeping, something I seldom did before. And I came to realize how much of what consumes our daily life truly is trivial and insignificant."

His statement reminded me of a much earlier conversation, not long after he came to Chicago. He had visited Misericordia South, a facility for the severely retarded. At Misericordia, the residents suffer devastating disabilities. "I almost cried," he told me some time after. The message was clear. He wasn't uncaring or insensitive. It's just that bishops didn't cry. It is seen as a sign of weakness. Now, years later, he was given the gift of tears.

Just a few weeks before the press conference at which he would announce his terminal illness, the cardinal had announced that he was facing back surgery. He stated that the problems he was experiencing with his lower spine were not a direct result of the cancer surgery but were related to it. Three vertebrae in his lower back had been "crushed." There was evidence of osteoporosis, aggravated by the chemotherapy. He was in considerable pain and had been forced to use a walking stick.

One evening, while preparing for a trip, he took a fall on the stairs in his huge, seventeen-chimney gingerbread mansion. He had to crawl along the wide corridors of the 111-year-old house to Msgr. Kenneth Velo's quarters in order to seek help from his former executive assistant, who is now the president of the Catholic Church Extension Society.

Examination revealed that there was evidence of osteoporosis and a stenosis — or constriction — in his back. After visits to specialists, including a helicopter flight to Madison, Wisconsin, it was decided that he would undergo back surgery to relieve the pressure. The operation was the subject of another press conference in which he announced that the back surgery would be performed on September 16, and that he would be hobbled for about six weeks.

The cardinal wasn't looking forward to the surgery but was satisfied that his cancer was in remission and that the aching back was simply a necessary adjustment. So he took to his cane, turning it into an ice breaker at social and religious events, putting it aside only during liturgies. At public dinners, he would hold his stick up next to his podium and joke about his need of it. (Once, at an audience with John Paul II, it was reported that the pope had said: "So, Joseph, you're using a cane. So am I.")

Bernardin likes nice things. His newly acquired stick was a good example of this. He wouldn't have purchased the ninety-year-old, gold-handled, black-stained stick, but he was proud of this beautifully crafted one that his friend, Matt Lamb, a successful funeral director turned painter, had given him.

"Look," he said to me one day. "It's dated 1906." The cardinal had an eye for quality. He enjoyed wearing a well-made episcopal ring, sometimes preferring it to the one John Paul II had given each of his cardinals. He had a drawer filled with rings, most belonging to his predecessors. ("That's good," a psychologist friend of mine observed. "A little hedonism is good for the soul.")

✠

An unusual number of priests died during the winter of 1995 and spring of 1996. It is a sacred custom that the ordinary attend the funerals of his priests. The absence of the ordinary without a well-publicized reason can reflect displeasure with the deceased's life. If he couldn't attend, the cardinal would call the family personally to offer his condolences. Bernardin attended faithfully, although it often meant considerable juggling of his schedule.

At funerals following his cancer surgery, just before the final blessing, the cardinal would put his cane aside and walk somewhat awkwardly across the sanctuary. It was clear that he was in pain. Yet, he would always have done his homework. He always knew something of the priest's life and work and he would never talk about himself at such times. It was amazing how many priests he had come to know during his Chicago years. Many

of those he was blessing had retired years before he came to
Chicago.

The priests appreciated the gesture, although some would
complain that he seldom stayed around after the funeral for the
traditional rolled ham and potato salad luncheon in the church
basement. Again, there was his frantic schedule, but there was
also the fact that, while Bernardin loved his priests and was
more comfortable with them than with lay people, he had a
natural reserve that he rarely set aside. Most likely, he found
it easier to quietly leave as soon as the body was placed in the
hearse.

Many of his fellow bishops travel in posses, surrounded by
clerical aides who run interference for them. One can rarely get
near them. But Bernardin often drove alone or with his friend,
Fr. Velo, in his gray Buick to one of his nearly 400 parishes and
480 other institutions. At such gatherings, he often had to make
his way among priests he barely knew and laity whom he didn't
know at all. Yet, even when his back so limited him that he had
to reduce his schedule, he asked his staff not to cut back on his
appearances at large gatherings. He liked such occasions. They
seemed to fire him up.

At one gathering early in his administration, he handed me his
topcoat and plunged into the crowd, shaking hands with everyone. He appeared embarrassed when people tried to kiss his ring,
but he didn't stop them. He understood the frail packages in
which faith is carried.

✠

By 1:00 p.m., TV trucks filled one side of Superior Street.
Camera crews were unloading the bulky equipment that would
virtually fill the press room, leaving only two rows of seats for
the on-camera reporters and print media, many of whom had
microphones or tape cassettes.

Modern press conferences are technical marvels, although they can so intrude upon the speaker that he or she becomes intimidated. The cardinal's lectern was topheavy with cords and microphones. Later, in the press conference, the cardinal would have to compete with TV reporters who were broadcasting live within a dozen feet of him, even as he read his statement. Civility had given way to urgency.

Television people were admitted first — an irritant to the print media. The rationale is that they must set up their equipment and test dozens of buttons. It means, however, that a Peter Steinfels, senior religion writer for the *New York Times,* must cool his heels outside. Steinfels, who is steeped in his subject, waited patiently with his wife, Margaret O'Brien Steinfels, editor of *Commonweal,* a distinguished lay Catholic weekly. Both were in town for a book conference. They would write thoughtful comments while the TV reporters were often limited to twenty seconds of film. The massive cyclops of television had turned reporting into an uneven playing field.

The technical equipment was a measure of the importance of the conference. It underscored another impact that the Chicago cardinal has had. Many bishops have only a distant and strained relationship with the media. Some, borrowing on the customs of old, view themselves as royalty, not required to answer questions from the peasants. Others simply issue releases that spell out what they want reported, but they never answer questions. Some releases open with "His eminence decrees...."

All this is especially true when a scandal crashes through the stained-glass windows of a once imperial church. "With some of the bishops, it's a four-step process," one press veteran said. "First, complete denial, combined with criticism of the media. Then, a partial denial combined with the same criticism.

"When the evidence piles up," he continued, "there's a partial admission coupled with the same criticism. Finally, they tell the truth."

One of Bernardin's significant contributions was a change in the policies regarding the media. Soon after he arrived in Chicago, he held a press conference that was striking for its openness.

It was my first experience in covering a prince of the church. When it ended, I was invited to be part of an evening discussion on WGN Radio, a fifty-thousand-watt AM station owned by the powerful Tribune company. During the discussion breaks, I asked a seasoned reporter his view of the earlier conference. He responded: "Good, especially if he [Bernardin] was telling the truth."

I was shocked. Archbishops didn't lie. However, after seventeen years of John Patrick Cody's reign, the press had become hardened. Especially during his final years, the erratic and often imperial careerist cardinal had battled with the press. He actually engaged a public relations firm whose sole task, it seemed, was to ferret out media sins, including counting the number of times in which the Catholic Church was cast in a negative light.

Although the charges were never proven, Cody had spent his final months in office denying reports of federal charges of corruption involving the misuse of archdiocesan monies. He viewed himself as a "corporation sole." Indeed, he was. Legally, he owned the Chicago archdiocese and did not have to account for its monies. Questions as to how he distributed the funds were viewed as challenges to his authority.

Following his death, the *Chicago Sun-Times,* which had exposed the alleged scandal, locked up the evidence and the federal government quietly backed off. But the odor of suspicion remained. Bernardin had to deal with a press that had lost its faith.

"I can't pretend to understand him," Bernardin would say later. "I was only three years old when he was ordained." Years later, when he faced death himself, Cardinal Bernardin told me: "In 1988 I visited the Bishops' Mausoleum at Mount Carmel Ceme-

tery. I was asked to pick my spot. I selected one to the left of
Cardinal Cody. I suppose that I've always been a little to his left."

✠

Joseph Louis Bernardin set a new style for communications. He
rarely made any significant decision without considering how
such decisions would be carried to the media. I once encountered him walking to an important meeting on the subject of
gays in the Chicago church. He was alone and, as always, in
somewhat of a hurry. He was carrying a good-sized bundle of
press releases. He didn't offer me one. That would have put
the announcement ahead of the meeting. The cardinal could be
terminally prudent.

Now the ailing cardinal entered the press room near the end of
a thin procession of five of his auxiliary bishops and a half-dozen
of his staff. He viewed the crowd, many of whom were sitting
on the floor against the wall. With a faintly melancholic smile,
he observed: "Next time we'll use the United Center." (The huge
United Center had just been the site of the Democratic Convention. Bernardin had been asked to give the invocation to open
the convention, but he declined, in part to express his disap-
pointment with a recently vetoed bill that would bar late-term
abortions. "I like President Clinton," he told me. "But we cannot
have late-term abortions.")

The cardinal is a strong pro-life advocate but because he extends the issue to embrace all life, he is viewed as weak on
abortion. Many pro-life advocates limit the issue to the pre-born.
Even during the period of his illness, he was criticized for not
picketing outside the Democratic Convention or at the Sheraton
Hotel where President Clinton was staying. "I'm in a lose-lose
situation," he said often.

He addressed the reporters: "I have been told that the cancer
has returned, this time in the liver. I have been told that it is

terminal and my life expectancy is one year or less. I will begin a
different form of chemotherapy entitled Gemzar (gemcitabine).
If successful, this therapy may increase my time somewhat but
will not effect a cure."

One broadcaster started his sound byte immediately, turning
his back on the cardinal and talking into his network's camera.
The cardinal gave a faintly wistful look and went on with his
statement: "In the light of this latest diagnosis the back surgery
for the spinal stenosis has been canceled. Such surgery is usually
done only when the prospects for life are more promising."

Five of his auxiliary bishops — two of them retired — formed
the background to the podium. On the far left, Bishop Raymond E. Goedert, vicar general of the archdiocese, leaned one
shoulder against the wall. Goedert had administered the archdiocese during Bernardin's absence for his surgery. He would
administer the archdiocese again during the period before and
after the cardinal's death. He lives at the cardinal's mansion, and
the two priests had become quite close. Goedert, a former president of the sixteen-hundred-member Canon Law Society of
America and past officer of the Association of Chicago Priests,
a group that was founded during the Cody years in an effort
to penetrate the episcopal door to Cody's mind, is respected
by the Chicago clergy. He is viewed as a plainspoken, honest
Luxembourg-American, but is clearly a man of deep feelings. It
was reported that he "really lost it" when informed of Bernardin's
fatal illness. Now he would have even more duties as he assisted
the cardinal through his final illness. There were even rumors
that he might succeed him, although an auxiliary bishop rarely
makes the leap to archbishop-cardinal.

Across the room, John H. White, a Pulitzer Prize-winning
photographer for the *Chicago Sun-Times*, sagged against the wall.
He was overcome with emotion. White had first met the cardinal in 1979 at a New York airport ceremony welcoming Pope
John Paul II to the U.S. He snapped his first picture of him

that day and continued to take pictures of him for the next seventeen years. In the process the son of an African-American minister and the Italian-American cardinal became good friends. The cardinal occasionally called him with exclusives — inviting him, for example, to take pictures in his hospital room following his surgery. (The result was a 186-page book of black and white pictures, titled *This Man Bernardin* which White produced with Eugene Kennedy.)

"No one told me that he was going to die," White told me after another press conference following Bernardin's visit to Italy. "I had a front-row seat in his life. He is a great man."

After Bernardin's funeral, during a special liturgy for the media, John White delivered a brief, touching commendation. "With my camera, I captured his life," White said. "With his life, he captured my heart."

"I have been assured that I still have some quality time left," Bernardin continued. "My prayer is that I will use whatever time is left in a positive way, that is, a way that will be of benefit to the priests and people I have been called to serve, as well as to my own spiritual well-being."

✠

In the fourteen months since Bernardin's cancer had been diagnosed his life — and lifestyle — had changed dramatically. The cardinal had lived in a busy and often fiercely political world. He was bishop to 988 diocesan priests alone, each of whom had been educated to think of their ordinary as their spiritual father. In addition there were 861 religious priests, 587 permanent deacons, 3,574 sisters, and 457 brothers. They work in over 800 institutions that are tied in some way to the Pastoral Center.

Understandably, access to the cardinal was limited. Visits were carefully scheduled, and, generally speaking, one got an appointment only after the petitioner's intentions were clearly defined. Most appeals were assigned to other members of his cabinet or staff. I once asked for an hour for a book I was doing. He booked me himself for his home on a Saturday morning. When it was over, he reminded: "Well, Tim, you asked for an hour and I gave you two." He needed to measure his time.

However, months before, at the Loyola Cancer Treatment Center attached to Loyola University Hospital in Maywood, Illinois, the rhythm of his life had changed dramatically. Suddenly, he was surrounded with people who didn't have appointments — fellow patients with no agenda, who wanted nothing of him other than to share the experience of their cancer.

His room at Loyola had been inundated with flowers, enough to bury a monarch. He asked that they be distributed to the other patients. The flowers immediately established a link, and during his recovery days at the center that would soon be named after him, he walked the halls, meeting other patients who were taking their first tentative steps.

The ubiquitous television sets in the hospital rooms also introduced him to other patients even before he met them. One patient, a little non-Catholic girl, saw him so often on TV that she finally ordered her mother: "Hey, go get me that pope man!" (They did meet and became friends. The girl's leukemia is now in remission.)

The hospital experience caused Bernardin to change his priorities. "I felt like a priest again," he told me, a statement he would repeat often. In the year that followed, his prayer list reached six hundred fellow cancer sufferers. "I tell them to place themselves entirely in the hands of the Lord," he told the hard-nosed reporters at the press conference. "I have personally always tried to do that. Now I have done so with greater conviction than ever before."

Bernardin had a long-time habit of promising prayers. "If he named everyone he had promised to pray for in his morning

Mass," one priest-friend observed, "he would never get through the Mass!"

His spiritual therapy worked wonders with his fellow patients. Bernardin didn't cure anyone's cancer. "I don't believe in those kinds of miracles," he told me. But he lifted spirits and eased pain. He performed moral miracles. He persuaded people to prayer for each other and that each person's life is of infinite value.

A few weeks before Bernardin died, I attended a wake of an old woman who had been one of the cardinal's six hundred fellow sufferers. Next to her casket, the family had placed a framed picture of a touching letter she had received from him. It was not a brief note, nor did it read like a "canned" letter, produced by a computer. It cheered eighty-nine-year-old Hilda McGarry even more than one of the gooey papal blessings so readily available at shops surrounding the Vatican. It was already a family icon. Hilda's daughter, Mary Hartman, began carrying the letter around the large funeral parlor, showing it to all callers.

✠

During the year that followed his surgery, the cardinal had shared one thought with other cancer patients. Now, he wanted to share it with the media. It proved to be the most quoted portion of his statement:

"We can look at death as an enemy or a friend," he said. "If we see it as an enemy, death causes anxiety and fear. We tend to go into a state of denial. But if we see it as a friend, our attitude is truly different. As a person of faith," he continued, "I see death as a friend, as a transition from earthly life to life eternal."

It was the most unusual statement anyone could remember. A leader was announcing his death in the near future. Afterward, seasoned writers recalled that even the popes had never made statements like this. Generally, there is strong denial, coupled with implied criticism of the very physicians who are attending the bishop. In other cases there is a recognition that the situation is serious but that a loving God would spare the victim. In fact even as Bernardin spoke, the Vatican was assuring everyone that John Paul II was in excellent condition in spite of chronic problems. "A pope is never sick until he is dead," one reporter recalled. Bernardin was playing no such games. He viewed physicians as God's instruments. He trusted their judgments.

Cardinal Bernardin concluded his statement by asking the press to say a prayer for him — another innovation. There was a respectful silence for a moment; then the questions started.

One young reporter asked: "If you knew about this on Wednesday, why did you wait until now [Friday afternoon] to tell us?"

The veteran reporters moaned. "It's questions like that that give us a bad name," an experienced reporter observed.

Bernardin winced a bit, then answered patiently: "I needed time to notify my family, my staff, my fellow bishops, and my friends."

"How will you spend the time the doctors have given you?" another reporter asked. He answered that he would try to be more loving, more caring, and more compassionate. There was no talk of authority.

In the months that had preceded Bernardin's announcement there had been a great deal of speculation about his future. While few were willing to speak about his passing, it wasn't hard to find a conversation about his possible retirement or the appointment of a coadjutor archbishop who would share his duties and automatically succeed to the local throne when he retired or passed away.

Under John Paul II, coadjutor bishops were making a comeback. It is virtually impossible to unseat a bishop except for moral turpitude of some kind. In recent years two American archbishops — one in Atlanta and another in Santa Fe — had been forced to resign their posts because of admitted sexual indiscretions. But no one had a coadjutor forced upon him without his permission. Now, however, the Vatican had appointed coadjutors in Providence, St. Paul-Minneapolis, Dubuque, Seattle, and San Francisco. Vatican watchers saw it as a way for a conservative pope and an even more conservative curia to consolidate their power, even after the pope's passing. A coadjutor in Chicago would be a cardinal in storage — another conservative vote for the next pope.

The U.S. has ten American cardinals eligible to vote for a new pope. Nine of them are considered conservative, likely to vote for a fellow conservative. Only Bernardin could be expected to cast his ballot for a moderate. Although a cardinal for fourteen years, voting for a pope was a privilege he had never enjoyed.

Except in rare circumstances, the Vatican cannot remove a sitting bishop without his consent. Bernardin's predecessor, John Patrick Cody, had spent virtually every waking moment of his final years fighting off a Vatican that wanted desperately to replace him. They got nowhere.

Bernardin had no such cloud over him. While his health was poor, his mind was better than ever. He was feeling really at home in Chicago. Further, he had six auxiliary bishops to whom he could turn for help. The only advantage a coadjutor could offer would be that the cardinal would have the right of first refusal on Rome's choices. It was an option he didn't relish. He had witnessed other coadjutors being appointed, virtually none of them welcome choices.

On the heels of Bernardin's announcement, it seemed almost tacky to ask about a coadjutor. Only a few reporters had the necessary background for posing such a question. Some, in fact, were referring to the auxiliary bishops in the background as "Mister."

The first to raise the question was a seasoned reporter who first apologized for asking. The cardinal took the question without offense, answering simply that it was "premature" to talk about a coadjutor. He added, as he had on numerous occasions in the previous year, that if he felt the need for a coadjutor, he would ask for one.

The conference ended shortly after. The reporters simply couldn't find questions to ask. It was a sure bet that not one of them had covered a conference at which a prominent figure had announced his own death.

✠

Before turning off their cameras, the TV reporters turned to Eugene Kennedy and me for background bytes. Kennedy is a retired Loyola University psychology professor and the author of over forty books, many dealing with priesthood. He had completed one biography of Bernardin and had provided captions and background material for the aforementioned coffee table book he did with photographer John White. Kennedy assured the reporters that it wasn't maudlin to speak of Bernardin's successor, but he offered no names. (Later, he would mention Donald Wuerl, bishop of Pittsburgh.)

Outside the Pastoral Center, I was more forthcoming, but much less prudent than Gene Kennedy. I was offering names even as I recalled Msgr. John J. Egan's warning: "Listen, Tim. When Cody was appointed, the archdiocese had been vacant for months, and no one had even mentioned his name."

During the preceding year, I had often flipped through the Catholic Almanac and the massive Official Catholic Directory as well as the episcopal seniority lists issued by the National Conference of Catholic Bishops. Cardinal Bernardin was listed as the senior active American cardinal, archbishop of the second largest diocese in the U.S. (Los Angeles boasts over 3.5 million Catholics but has one hundred fewer churches and six hundred fewer priests.) He served on at least seven committees of the National

Conference and clearly was the best known of the 448 American cardinals, archbishops, and bishops. While technically the Vatican can pick a simple priest and catapult him to an archbishopric, such an event would be highly unlikely. Further, the long episcopal list pares down very easily once the cardinals, retired archbishops and bishops, auxiliary bishops (not likely to leapfrog to a cardinalate see), and those serving outside the country are eliminated.

Among the recurring names were Daniel Pilarczyk of Cincinnati, Anthony Pilla of Cleveland, Thomas Murphy of Seattle, Justin Rigali of St. Louis, and Donald Wuerl of Pittsburgh. All would be given a few seconds of fame on TV that evening. But their names would fade almost as quickly as they appeared, even as new ones surfaced.

✠

In spite of all the watered silk, rings, miters, and crosiers, the reality is that most Catholics barely know their local bishop. One newspaper poll had demonstrated that in one major archdiocese the cardinal archbishop had only a 20 percent name recognition rate.

Fr. Andrew M. Greeley, a Chicago priest, sociologist, and author of some 150 books, may be better known than most local bishops. The media turn to him on virtually every issue, partly because he knows his trade and has a unique ability to articulate issues. On television the evening the press conference closed, Greeley appeared pessimistic. He saw the Vatican appointing an authoritarian, a lackey for the powerful Eastern cardinals in Boston, New York, Philadelphia, Washington, and Detroit. (Only Cardinal William Keeler of Baltimore displayed some moderate gifts.) He named no one. Indeed, he may have shocked some by his frankness. But there were priests who shared his view.

"I've got a knot in my stomach," one priest said. "Joe's the best that's out there."

"Oh, let them appoint a hard-noser," another pastor said. "I'll just go on running this parish the way I have under Bernardin. If the new guy gives me a hard time, I'll just hand him the keys."

The cardinal was under no obligation to ask for a coadjutor. The Vatican would likely give him one if he asked, but they could control the choice. Further, given the relatively short time the cardinal had remaining, they could wait it out. At the time of his press conference at least seven dioceses were awaiting new bishops, three of them for over a year.

I received one letter and telephone call insisting that I be "a point man" on the question of lay involvement in the choice of a new archbishop. It is an idea so far removed from present political realities that it may be generations of bishops away. Not even the local clergy would be consulted on the appointment. Power like that simply isn't shared.

The sad reality is that even an immensely popular man like Joseph Bernardin has only a little impact on the lives of the faithful. His greatest impact would come in the final weeks of his life. Measurable influence pretty much ends with the local pastor — and that only for the approximately 25 percent of Chicago Catholics who attend church regularly. The thousands of Catholics and non-Catholics in the archdiocese would eventually know more about the state of his health than about his moral or spiritual influence.

✠

The conference ended in under thirty minutes. Gradually, the street outside the Pastoral Center began to clear. Soon there was only the cardinal's car. He left the building with two aides and quietly drove away after one of the most dramatic press conferences in the history of the Chicago church.

— TWO —

Getting to Know
a Cardinal

I FIRST MET Cardinal Joseph Bernardin in 1976, backstage at Chicago's Auditorium Theater. It was DePaul University's commencement day and the now sixteen-thousand-student university was granting the archbishop of Cincinnati an honorary degree.

At that time, I was director of alumni relations at DePaul and my boss, the late Arthur J. Schaefer, vice-president for development, alumni, and public relations, had asked me to represent him on the awards committee. We agreed to press Bernardin's candidacy because it seemed obvious even then that he would succeed the embattled Cardinal John Cody. As things turned out, Bernardin would not take over the depressed archdiocese for another six years.

Cardinal Cody was cut from a different cloth. A native of St. Louis, he had entered the seminary at only thirteen. By the time he was twenty-five, he was vice-rector of the North American College in Rome and a member of the Secretariat of State directed by Cardinal Eugenio Pacelli (later Pius XII). There he met a papal diplomat named Giovanni Montini, who would become Paul VI and would later hesitate to remove Cody from office. Cody knew how to throw Paul VI off base. He liked to remind him that he was a bishop seven years before Montini himself was. Cody also knew how to push buttons. With his famous $1,000 Mass Cards and other gifts, he had built a support system in Rome. Joseph Bernardin was a man much closer in spirit to Paul VI than to John Paul II. Cody clearly preferred John Paul II.

Paul VI died in August 1978. His successor, John Paul I, would die just seven weeks later, allegedly with papers near his bedside that would have sealed Cody's removal. His support of Cardinal Karol Wojtyla's candidacy and his elaborate treatment of John Paul II during his visit to Chicago in 1979 assured Cody's continuance in office until his death in 1982.

Before Chicago, Cody served in three dioceses as coadjutor to aging bishops. He arrived in Chicago after a carefully staged train ride with thousands of priests, sisters, and school children cheering him and politicians filling his private train car.

(It was in great contrast to Bernardin's quiet arrival at O'Hare Airport. His was not without fanfare. The auxiliary bishops and others were lined up to greet the new archbishop as he left the plane. However, Fr. John Jamnicky, chaplain at O'Hare, used his clout with airline officials. He entered the rear of the plane the minute it reached the gate and walked off the plane with the new archbishop.)

Cardinal Cody immediately set about shoring up the central bureaucracy of the archdiocese. He was a micro-manager, insisting upon signing virtually every check, often in the presence of a troubled priest who had come to see him, admonishing the priest with a "Can't you see I'm busy, Father?"

In fairness to the cardinal about whom every priest in Chicago had a story, he accomplished some things well. He raised millions for parish and school improvements, instituted health and life insurance plans for the clergy and lay employees, reorganized the major seminary, promoted the ordination of married men as permanent deacons, implemented the liturgical reforms of Vatican II, renovated his wedding cake cathedral in accordance with the new liturgy, and supported civil rights. However, according to historian Edward R. Kantowicz, his imperial style chilled both clergy and laity. In an institution where it is essential to be either loved or respected the embattled cardinal was neither. Sometime after being named a cardinal in 1967, Cody learned that Paul VI had abandoned the wide-brimmed red hats that were hung from the ceilings of cardinals' cathedrals. In a typical Cody reaction, he ordered one anyway and had it hung. Paul VI simply wanted to simplify the ceremonial garb of popes and cardinals; so the hat, called a galero, was replaced by a square-cornered red biretta. The smaller, simpler hat became a logo for Bernardin, part of a poster for his successful Big Shoulders campaign, and it rested on his cathedral chair during his funeral. In 1993 Fr. Thomas Paprocki, archdiocesan chancellor, and a group of priest friends ordered a galero for Bernardin from Gammarelli's clerical tailoring in Rome. They gave it to the cardinal as a gift. On December 14, a month after he died, it was hung in Holy Name Cathedral with the four other galeros.

For poor Cardinal Cody the priesthood was a career; for Cardinal Bernardin it was a vocation.

✠

Archbishop Bernardin knew the temperature in Chicago. As soon as his honorary degree was announced, Cody had called him and asked rhetorically: "You're not going to accept it, are you?"

Although the university had conferred an honorary degree upon him, Cody's relationship with DePaul had been strained. Technically, he was chancellor of the university, a largely honorary title, generally reserved to former presidents. When the late Fr. Comerford J. O'Malley, C.M., resigned as president, however, he was named chancellor and the archbishop was given the amorphous title of "Grand Chancellor," a designation not likely to allow him the privilege of a university library card. In addition there had been conflict regarding certain teachings within DePaul's theology department. DePaul had hired the brilliant and controversial John L. McKenzie, a former Jesuit and priest of the diocese of Madison, Wisconsin, and an acerbic columnist. They also had a number of other Scripture scholars with nontraditional views. Cody saw himself — correctly according to canon law — as the chief teacher of theology within his archdiocese. He regarded these faculty appointments as a challenge to his authority and a reflection upon himself. As with most authoritarian leaders, he tended to believe the first rumor that crossed his desk, and there was no shortage of letters from wounded conservatives. Further, it was a climate in which a priest could be disciplined for appearing on a television talk show in coat and tie, not to mention with a quiver filled with controversial theology or Scripture scholarship. Under Bernardin, the responsibility for maintaining a balance between theological correctness and academic freedom was delegated to the presidents of the respective seminaries and universities.

✠

Archbishop Bernardin arrived behind the auditorium stage, alone and looking a bit lost. I was standing there, trying to look important, although I had no specific duties. I was wallpaper.

He walked up to me, asking where to go to get into his episcopal robes. The other degree recipients and the university's top officials were in a separate room behind the stage. I walked the archbishop to the room while we chatted. I was immediately taken by his candor. "He [Cody] didn't want me to accept this," he said to me, likely thinking that I was a higher-ranking official than reality dictated. "But I told him that I was coming anyway."

Bernardin was politically shrewd. He had some sense that he might someday succeed to Chicago. Undoubtedly, he knew that, while Cody objected, his influence in Rome and with his fellow American bishops was on the wane.

By 1976, Bernardin had been president of the National Conference of Catholic Bishops for two years. Further, he had been general secretary of the conference from 1968 until his appointment as archbishop of Cincinnati in 1972. If push came to shove, Bernardin could measure Cody's influence precisely. Besides, Joseph Bernardin genuinely enjoyed receiving such awards. Somewhere inside him, the little Italian-American kid from Columbia, South Carolina, had an emotional center that took great pleasure in receiving awards. It's not that he lusted after them, only that he enjoyed the experience of getting them. (Allegedly, when first named a bishop in 1968, then the youngest bishop in the country, his mother, Maria Bernardin, cautioned him to "walk straight and try not to smile too much" as he walked down the cathedral aisle.)

Archbishop Bernardin returned to Cincinnati and into his third and final year as president of the National Conference of Catholic Bishops. The conference had been completely reorganized during his years as general secretary and, later, his three-year term as president. Ironically, it was undergoing still another reorganization in 1996 when Bernardin, still chairman of the Committee on Mission and Structure, was calling for a proposal that would merge the two conferences — the National Conference of Catholic Bishops and the United States Catholic Conference — into a single unit to be titled the U.S. Conference of Catholic Bishops, or USCCB. Bernardin was expected to be at the Omni Shoreham in Washington to lead the support for this proposal, but, just a week before the conference got underway, his office announced that his failing health would not permit his attendance. The news caused immediate concern. It was a measure of his influence. Several conservative bishops, led by Archbishop William Levada of San Francisco, were said to be planning to speak against the merger and to reintroduce the closed sessions that once marked the semiannual meetings. The conservatives claimed that outsiders — read laity and press — were inhibiting the genuine responses of the bishops. Bernardin, who had spent years fighting for a "sunshine" rule, had hoped to attend the 1996 meeting and to lead the fight for the continued inclusion of the laity. Although a cleric to his bones, he believed that good shepherds did not need fences between hierarchy and laity. He was deeply disappointed that he could not attend this final meeting of the organization he had structured.

✠

In any case, following the DePaul commencement, Bernardin would wait six more years before returning to Chicago as the newly appointed archbishop. In the meantime Paul VI, who had appointed John Patrick Cody to Chicago and Joseph Louis Bernardin to Cincinnati, would die of a heart attack on August 6, 1978. He had hesitated about the removal of Cody from office. Among the 144 cardinals he named during his sixteen years as pope was Cardinal Cody. It isn't easy to contradict one's own appointments.

Paul VI was succeeded by John Paul I, who had been elected on the fourth ballot by 111 cardinals — one of the largest and shortest conclaves in history. Sadly, the quickness of the election of "the smiling pontiff" was matched by the brevity of his pontificate of thirty-three days, during which he delivered nineteen addresses and, allegedly, considered the removal of Cardinal Cody from office. He died in bed of a heart attack on September 28, 1978.

Two weeks later, nearly the same 111 cardinals gathered under Michelangelo's famous ceiling in the Sistine Chapel and on the seventh or eighth ballot on October 16, 1978, the second day of voting, elected Karol Wojtyla of Krakow as bishop of Rome.

He was the first Polish pope in the history of the church and the first non-Italian since Adrian VI (1522–23). He was also the youngest pope since Pius IX (1846–78) and had received his red hat in 1967 at the same conclave as John Patrick Cody.

Within a year, John Paul II would visit Chicago. Cody spread a welcome mat that virtually covered Chicago. The pope made some fourteen appearances in just two days. By some reports, Cody spent in excess of $1,000,000 preparing Grant Park alone. It became clear that he would remain in office until his mandatory retirement of seventy-five.

Cardinal Cody died at seventy-four in April of 1982. In less than four months, on July 10, 1982, Bernardin was appointed directly by John Paul II. In less than six months he was a cardinal. It was clear that the Vatican wanted to erase memories of Cardinal Cody's erratic reign as quickly as possible.

Prior to and during the *interregnum,* there were rumors that Bernardin was part of a plot to overthrow Cody. The rumors died as soon as he was appointed, but they must have hurt him. Later, when I asked him about that period, he simply shook his head.

Not long before his appointment, Jean and I went shopping on Chicago's near north side. We parked just a few blocks from the Chicago chancery and Holy Name Cathedral, the parish church for the whole archdiocese. We went to one of our favorite delis and enjoyed an obscene pastrami and Swiss sandwich that likely took care of our fat intake for the new few days. Even as we gnawed at the pink pile of highly seasoned and smoked shoulder beef, Jean pointed to a cleric who was patiently waiting on line to place his order.

"Do you know who that is?" she asked. I didn't but she quickly informed me that it was the Episcopal bishop of Chicago. We marveled at how another church leader could mingle with ordinary people. We complained to each other that our church leaders had grown so remote that the notion of a cardinal —

even a lowly auxiliary bishop — on line in a grubby deli was simply out of the question.

The subject was forgotten as we clogged our arteries, but still later, as I passed the Pastoral Center, I spotted the priest who was administering the archdiocese during the brief period between Cody's death and Bernardin's arrival. Msgr. Richard Keating was leaving in a chauffeured car, something Cody had used for several years prior to his death. Keating was a young man, a French-cuffed careerist, but one fully capable of driving his own car. (He is now bishop of Arlington, Virginia.) The picture burned a hole in me. I asked why the functionary, who had angered a few auxiliary bishops when they were passed over as interim administrators, was being driven. I was informed that the archdiocese was a corporation sole, a legal term that meant simply that the archbishop was the sole officer of the corporation and that the archbishop literally owned the archdiocese. (On occasion, Cody was known to say: "What do you mean? I own this archdiocese!") The legalism translated to the chauffeured car. It meant that if the archbishop or his stand-in caused an accident, some sharp lawyer, observing the vast assets of the archdiocese, could sue for millions.

✠

I found myself growing increasingly obsessed by the politics of ecclesiastical life, the dangerously low morale of the clergy, and the growing financial scandal within the archdiocese. During an idle moment at my job at Northwestern University, I began a letter to the still unnamed archbishop. The letter grew to at least seven typewritten pages. It was therapeutic for me. I poured my anger onto each page.

I showed the letter to Jean. She had long known of both my interest in the politics of church and in writing. I had written for years, largely for others. They were commencement and dinner speeches, brochures, reports, foundation proposals, and a flood of letters on behalf of my university superiors. In part this windy letter sprang from sheer practice effect. Words came easily, especially when fueled with anger.

The letter was partly tongue-in-cheek. It began by suggesting that the new archbishop go to the deli and get a take-out sandwich and that he bring it to the park near the chancery and eat it there while he talked with the people who filled the benches and the lawn of the little park. I then suggested that he walk to work or simply take a bus from his nearby mansion. Later, I asked that he sell the mansion and move to a more modest house, closer to the chancery.

The cardinal's mansion was located on the edge of Lincoln Park. It had been built by Archbishop Patrick A. Feehan, who headed the archdiocese from 1880 to 1902. Feehan built the massive, seventeen-chimney Victorian house in 1885 as an "in-your-face" response to Chicago Protestants who lived in splendor just south of the mansion. Archdiocesan lore claims that Feehan co-opted the property from the Sisters of Mercy without compensating them. Thus, when talk of selling the mansion comes up, the explanation is that the archdiocese can't sell what it doesn't own. "Nonsense," one lawyer told me. "If the Sisters never bothered to exercise their ownership for over a century, the property now belongs to the archdiocese."

Whatever the case, the mansion, with its thirty-three rooms, remains a symbol of industrial age leadership. In my open letter to the new archbishop I called it "a haunted house, so spooky with clericalism, triumphalism, and a host of other ghosts." I pointed out that Playboy mogul Hugh Hefner had moved off North State Parkway, claiming that it was simply too expensive to maintain his mansion, which was about half the size of the cardinal's. Further, past bishops had made only a little use of the mansion. George Mundelein and Samuel Stritch preferred to live in a Monticello-type mansion on the seminary property at Mundelein. During Cody's time, he had turned some of its best rooms into offices with neon lighting. When he played host to John Paul II, it took a squad of hard-working Polish nuns to bring the house up to snuff. But selling the place would not be easy. Building codes passed to keep developers from overbuilding now reduced it to a single-use property.

It wasn't as if my suggestions went unheeded. Others had made them well before me. But Bernardin's real estate and financial advisors had told him that the mansion was basically an ecclesiastical elephant. At a modest $2.5 million, even Hefner could not sell his place. He ended up giving it to the School of the Art Institute. Today, it has been converted to condominiums.

The remainder of my letter suggested that the new archbishop unplug the Telex to the Vatican, open the archdiocesan stock portfolio to the Chicago church, remove the direct line phone to the archdiocesan lawyers' office, and direct his communications office to stop denying everything and to tell the truth.

I was just warming up. I told him to welcome resigned priests to his home, recall some truly significant priests who were living in exile because of conflicts with Cody, and, above all, start listening to his priests. I called for a black auxiliary and a Latino. I asked him to listen to the nuns who had been largely ignored throughout the history of the archdiocese. It was a long laundry list and yet one that was only partially complete.

At Jean's insistence, I sent the letter off to Michael Farrell, now senior editor of the *National Catholic Reporter.* Farrell put it on the front page of the lay-owned weekly that enjoys its position as the best of the more liberal and independent Catholic papers.

The lengthy epistle launched my freelance writing career. Within five years of its appearance, I resigned my position at Northwestern University and pursued full-time writing. Hundreds of articles and five books followed. And a peculiar but genuinely rewarding friendship developed with the man who unwittingly changed my professional — and spiritual — life.

The open letter was picked up by many secular papers; the diocesan papers ignored it. It also brought many letters. My advice was praised but also called "juvenile," "simplistic," and "condescending." And a copy was sent to Bernardin, who had been appointed to Chicago in the interim. His response was termed "abstract, nervous, sober, and censorious." His critique was a bit sharp. Bernardin could sometimes be vague and pedantic. He could not free himself from the bounds of prudence and the compulsion to be a teacher. My loosely written letter was clearly not in the style to which he had become accustomed.

However, Bernardin caught my underlying message. "The principal thrust of Mr. Unsworth's letter, as I perceived it, was that I should be a down-to-earth pastor, one who remains close to the people." He never did get to the deli, however. It closed not long after he arrived, making way for a fast food place that served borderline E-coli food. He did begin driving his own car, only to have me suggest to him later that he get a driver and a car phone because of the demands made on him and even the threats he received. For a time, he was stalked by at least one fanatic who lurked in Lincoln Park. On another evening, two Milwaukee police officers on a drunken spree in Chicago fired shots through his front door. (They later killed a young bouncer at a north side bar. Bernardin immediately called his widow.)

He never left the mansion. Instead, he cleaned it up, moved a few staff priests in, and used it for gatherings. Besides, he genuinely liked the place.

Years later, I would write a book that included a chapter on him. It was largely quotations from him, taken directly from tape. Yet, he needed to tighten up the dialogue, telling a mutual friend that "the comments were all over the place." The cardinal has been described as "obsessive-compulsive," a designation he freely admitted to. I once said to him that I had heard that he actually rewrites or at least edits even sixty-second invocations that he is asked to give at major dinners. "I do," he said. And over the years, I have seen him actually doing it moments before he was introduced to give the blessing. It was a byproduct of his obsessive prudence, another character trait to which he freely admitted. "I think I got it from my father," he said. "I barely remember him, but I'm told that he was a very prudent man."

✠

My first effort at Catholic journalism proved to be a lucky hit. The byline identified me as an employee of Northwestern University. The university's clipping service received some two hundred snippets of my letter, gleaned from a wide variety of secular papers. It also caused some nervous Northwestern administrators to fret about the possibility that my letter would cause bumper damage between the elite WASP university and the local church. One vice-president whom I somehow irritated immensely actually inquired as to whether or not I should be fired. (A university lawyer responded: "Not unless you want to be sued.") The very thought of being a martyr to my first article excited me.

Just before Christmas after Bernardin arrived, he held a reception at Quigley Seminary in order to meet the staff. At that time, my wife was a part-time consultant at the Archdiocesan School Board. She wondered in advance if she would meet him and whether or not he would make the connection.

He did.

"Are you Tim Unsworth's wife?" he asked. "Yes," she answered. "Give him my regards," he said. And she moved on.

Months later, Bernardin was a cardinal and already deeply involved in archdiocesan affairs. Jean was a member of the Art and Environment Commission which had resigned en masse under Cody. It was now being reconstituted at Bernardin's request. In the conference room at the Holy Name Cathedral rectory, Jean found herself at the cardinal's right hand. During the traditional wine and cheese break, he turned to Jean and said: "I want to talk to you about that letter."

Jean was apprehensive. She needn't have been. He told her that he thought the letter was so funny that he had brought it to a farewell party before leaving Cincinnati and read snippets of it aloud. Jean responded that she would love to have me meet the cardinal and he agreed. She invited him to dinner. A date was set a few days later and he came. It would be an annual event for the next fourteen years.

✠

Getting to know a cardinal can be a heady experience. Cardinals are a rare species. Their power as a group, first given to them by Pope Nicholas II, who died in 1061, has been limited to the privilege of electing a pope. In 1586 Pope Sixtus V set the maximum number at seventy, representing the seventy elders of Moses, but this limit was abrogated by John XXIII in 1958.

In 1962 John XXIII also ruled that all cardinals first be ordained bishops, and his successor, Paul VI, ruled that cardinals who reach their eightieth birthday lose their voting privilege. In 1973 he also set a limit of 120 on the number who could vote. According to the 1996 *Catholic Almanac*, there were 162 cardinals at the close of 1995. Over forty were over eighty and, given the age of many of them, they passed away at a steady rate.

Cardinal Bernardin genuinely wanted to exercise the privilege of voting for a pope. There was something in him that liked such rituals and protocols. Sadly, he never got a chance to cast a vote, although there were occasions during his tenure when the whole world watched as John Paul II seemed to be close to death. It may have been a relief to his fellow American cardinals. Bernardin told me that he would likely vote for Cardinal Carlo Maria

Martini, S.J., archbishop of Milan, and a moderate. He wasn't suggesting that Martini, a member of the world-renowned vermouth family, was his only candidate, just that he liked the tall, distinguished ordinary of a massive diocese. During the earlier years of Bernardin's cardinalate, there were often rumors that Bernardin himself would be a candidate for the papacy. The rationale among some was that the cardinals had made a big mistake in electing a hard-nosed, plainspoken Polish pope who ruled with a heavy hand. They needed to get the church back under the control of a more nuanced Italian pope. Since there were few eligible Italians, it was thought that a prudent Italian-American would be a good compromise.

Bernardin was flattered by such speculation but quickly dismissed it. "I don't even speak Italian," he would say, although he understands the language quite well and can get by speaking and reading it. In reality, the shrewd cardinal knew that Americans are simply not that well-liked worldwide and that he would not enjoy the support of the ten remaining eligible American cardinals, none of whom would likely vote for Martini or Bernardin.

✠

Cardinal Joseph Bernardin was the twenty-seventh American cardinal named since John McCloskey of New York received the red hat in 1875. He was Chicago's fifth cardinal, succeeding George Mundelein (1915–39), Samuel Stritch (1939–58), Albert Meyer (1958–65), and John Patrick Cody (1965–82). Mundelein received his red hat in 1924, making him the first cardinal not from the East Coast.

Cardinals from the East Coast still predominate, leading to the tart observation that they are "wise men from the East." They can presently be found in Boston, New York, Philadelphia, Baltimore, and Washington. Two more cardinals serve in Rome and another is in Detroit. The only cardinal west of Chicago is Roger M. Mahony of Los Angeles.

I have long had a fascination with prelates. It is seen as a character disorder by my friends. It may stem from the time I visited Franklin Field in Philadelphia to see Cardinal Dennis Dougherty (1918–51) process across the football field at some eucharistic congress to which the Catholic schoolchildren had been bused. His seventy-foot watered silk train, mounted by an ermine cape, was pretty impressive to this Depression-era kid. And when the stadium announcer proclaimed that "no one is to leave the stadium until His Eminence has disappeared," I thought that a chariot would arrive from the heavens to collect old Denny.

Years later, I would meet a few other cardinals and actually befriend Timothy Manning of Los Angeles, with whom I shared an interest in contemporary Irish literature. He was also very kind to me when I was installed into his predecessor's CCC (Cardinal's Carpet Club) for daring to hire a resigned priest to teach in one of the archdiocesan schools where I served as a vice-principal. The crusty Cardinal James McIntyre held resigned priests in low regard. He wanted the man fired but held off his orders until the end of the school year. Meanwhile, Cardinal Manning, then an auxiliary bishop, was quietly arranging a dispensation for the man so that he could marry in the church.

✠

Bernardin's first visit to our home was preceded by endless preparation. Try as we might, it was somewhat formal, even though he removed his clerical blacks, embraced Jean, and sat in our kitchen, sipping Campari, until the meal was ready.

After that, it was easy. The gentle prelate could calm lions.

— THREE —

The Path to Chicago

CARDINAL JOSEPH BERNARDIN'S biographer and close friend, Eugene Kennedy, has called him "the most influential bishop in the history of the American church." It was a sentiment that even more objective observers could also stand on.

The first Italian-American to head a major archdiocese, at the time of his death he was the senior active American bishop among the country's 350-plus bishops. But his influence far exceeded his seniority. His writing and speaking on national — even global — issues have caused him to eclipse mega-bishops such as Baltimore's James Gibbons (1877–1921), Boston's William O'Connell (1907–44), Chicago's George Mundelein (1915–39), New York's Francis Spellman (1939–67), and Bernardin's own mentor, John Dearden of Detroit (1958–80).

The earlier cardinals were churchmen for their times — builders and authoritarian princes. Bernardin set an entirely new style, one marked more by gentle leadership than feudal authority.

Nationally, Bernardin strongly influenced teaching on pro-life issues, nuclear weapons, the pursuit of peace, and equitable economic policy. As a national administrator, he supervised the reorganization of the National Conference of Catholic Bishops and was attempting to fine-tune the conference even more at the time of his death. He also served as a patient, consensus-building oil can to the sometimes squeaky machinery of church politics.

As a local ordinary, he developed new models for dealing with the politics of cutback, developing less painful ways of closing churches and schools. He also created models to deal with the even more painful problem of clerical sexual abuse. All the while, he attempted to form new models of dialogue with both priests and laity. While he didn't fully succeed, few bishops could match his example for listening, consulting, and building consensus.

✠

Joseph Louis Bernardin's career path had unlikely origins. Few major bishops have come out of the South. Few did not study at the North American College or one of the other Vatican-connected universities. Many hold degrees in canon law or Vatican-related doctorates which, in certain circumstances, are as easy to obtain as a Reno divorce. John Patrick Cody earned two doctorates in a single year. Ghostwritten dissertations were commonplace in some quarters. But the advanced degrees add a certain patina to a careerist's resumé. Bernardin, who would be weighted down with honorary degrees, had only one earned graduate degree — a master's in education. Yet he was more of a scholar than many of his episcopal colleagues.

Bernardin was a model of Aquinas's dictum that there are two kinds of knowledge: to know facts and to know where they are. He knew where it was and he didn't hesitate to call upon it to bring credibility to his writings.

Born in Columbia, South Carolina, on April 2, 1928, he was raised in a city that was then less than 2 percent Catholic. His native diocese, Charleston, still has only 120,000 Catholics, or 2.8 percent of the state's population.

His parents, Joseph, known as Beppi, and Maria (Simion) Bernardin were from the village of Tonadico in the valley of Primiero, located in the Dolomite mountains of northern Italy.

The village is so close to Austria that many locals consider themselves Austrians, although they speak Italian. In fact, Bernardin's father served in the Austro-Hungarian army before immigrating to the U.S. with his five brothers. The six master stonecutters tried Barre, Vermont, a major area for quarrying stone, but jobs were scarce. So they moved on.

Many of his relatives remained in Italy and, as Bernardin observed years later, "they may have prospered more than those who emigrated." According to him, they did well in the tourist business. Bernardin loved to visit the area and did so regularly from 1957 until a year before his death.

With two of his brothers, Joseph Bernardin went to Columbia to work in another quarry. In 1927 he returned to Tonadico with one of his brothers to marry Maria Simion at the church of St. Sebastian; Beppi's brother married Maria's sister. Even before returning to Italy, the older Bernardin had hints that he may have been in the early stages of cancer. The family returned to Columbia but, soon after, the future cardinal's father took ill. He died in 1934 when his son was barely six. Maria Bernardin had to work as a seamstress for the WPA (Work Projects Administration) to support her small family, which included her son and daughter, now Mrs. Elaine Addison of Columbia, South Carolina. Some accounts say that Maria made fine lace; another that she made army uniforms. For a time, she also ran a small grocery store not far from their home.

Bernardin attended both Catholic and public elementary schools, public high school, and, for one year, the University of South Carolina, where he was enrolled as a scholarship student in a pre-med program. Encouraged by other friends who had entered the seminary, he entered St. Mary's Seminary in Kentucky to study Latin for a year in order to prepare for the major seminary. At St. Mary's Seminary in Baltimore, he earned a B.A. (*summa cum laude*) in philosophy in 1948. In 1952 at Catholic University in Washington, D.C., he completed a master of arts in education. His superiors invited him to continue his education in Rome, but he refused, largely out of concern for his mother.

Bernardin's seminary classmates were a mixed group of some forty-six or forty-seven men, all but one of them older than he was. The only two to become bishops were the two youngest. (The other young man was George O. Wirz, now auxiliary bishop of Madison, Wisconsin.) Most were military veterans and college grads, including a lawyer, a journalist, a professor, and military officers.

Among his classmates was Frank Bonnike, now a resigned priest of the Rockford, Illinois, diocese. They remained good friends from those idyllic seminary days. "His room was just two doors down the hall," Bonnike recalled. "He shared a room with Freddy Bloom [now in Rockville, Maryland, in the archdiocese of Washington, D.C.]. Bloom is a kind of class secretary. He sends out two newsletters each year, and if you don't contribute something, Freddy will make up something terrible about you. Joe [Bernardin] always wrote something."

Bonnike remembers Bernardin as a down-to-earth, unassuming man with a "terrible southern accent." He often fretted about his grades, and, according to Bonnike, "he would then pull a 98."

The class was required to go out three afternoons each week in order to perform some corporal work of mercy. "I can't remember what Joe did," Bonnike said, "but it was likely just what we all did — some teaching, helping the poor or the elderly.

"I got in with some guys who wanted change," Bonnike recalled. "We often sat around, trying to think of ways to blow the place up. But Joe wasn't a part of that. Ironically, the leader of the bunch I got in with wound up a country pastor," he continued, "and Joe went on to become a real leader." Bonnike was not surprised when Bernardin became a bishop. "No one was surprised," he said. "It was a given."

Other observers recalled that there was something of a bureaucrat in the future cardinal, even in those days. Early on, it seems, Joe Bernardin was a careerist. Years later, speaking to his Chicago priests, he spoke quite poignantly of this tendency. "There were times in my life when I have made political decisions rather than priestly ones," he once told the presbyteral senate, "and now I regret it."

"When will you do this (or that)?" his classmates would challenge him. "When a'hm a bishop," he would say. "Then ah'll know what Jesus wants." Then his fellow seminarians would raise the ante through archbishop, cardinal, and pope. "And when you're pope?" they asked. "Will you know what Jesus wants?" And Bernardin would answer, "Yes, but I've got this College of Cardinals to deal with." It was a prophetic game.

"All that changed radically when he got to Cincinnati," Bonnike recalled. "He got in with a group of young priests and they taught him how to pray. He never gave up being a taskmaster, but in Cincinnati he became much more a people person."

On April 26, 1952, he was ordained at St. Joseph's Church, his home parish, in Columbia for the diocese of Charleston. He was assigned to that parish and to a teaching position at Bishop England High School, a school named for the first bishop of Charleston (1820–42).

Within two years, he was moved to the Charleston chancery office, where he performed a variety of tasks, including superintendent of cemeteries and chaplain to the Citadel.

Within seven years, he was named a papal chamberlain (Very Reverend Monsignor), and by 1962 John XXIII had appointed him a domestic prelate (Right Reverend Monsignor). In small dioceses advancement is often more rapid, if only because the pyramid is so small. But even in Charleston, Bernardin was moving swiftly.

✠

Advancement in the church relies heavily on a mentoring system, generally supported by connections in Rome. Bernardin became a philosophical and political disciple of the second of four Charleston bishops under whom he served. He was Paul Hallinan, a native of Cleveland, who was named bishop of Charleston in 1958, the year that Pius XII died.

Biographer Eugene Kennedy described Hallinan as "a man of great faith and optimism," two traits that Bernardin cultivated throughout his priesthood. "Defend the principle," Hallinan would tell him often. It was an axiom that Bernardin would abide by throughout his life. It was the "defense of the principle" that fueled his writings and teachings and kept him from wielding the hammer of episcopal authority.

In 1962 John XXIII appointed Hallinan as the first archbishop of Atlanta. Four years later, Bernardin would follow him there as an auxiliary bishop. He was only thirty-eight and the youngest bishop in the country.

Paul Hallinan's mentor was John Dearden of Detroit, a cardinal who had made a dramatic transition from the "Iron John" of Pittsburgh to a cardinal-archbishop of Detroit willing to carry out the mandates of the Second Vatican Council. The three men would occasionally vacation together, sharing prayers and thoughts.

After Hallinan became ill, Bernardin virtually administered the archdiocese until Hallinan's death in 1968. Bernardin did not succeed Hallinan into the rather small archdiocese (then 35,000; now nearly 200,000 Catholics). The job was filled by Francis E. Hyland through New York's Cardinal Spellman. Mentors occasionally run into other mentors.

By 1968, however, Cardinal Dearden was named president of the National Conference of Catholic Bishops. He asked that Bernardin be appointed general secretary. Dearden didn't want to spend too much time in Washington. He wanted a man he could trust to carry out his policies. It meant moving aside Francis T.

Hurley of San Francisco, who had served the conference since 1957. (He would later be named bishop of Juneau, Alaska, and in 1976 archbishop of Anchorage.) Bernardin had declined the position twice already but this time the pressure was increased.

Also in 1968 Paul VI's encyclical *Humanae Vitae* appeared and the National Federation of Priests Councils (NFPC) was formed. The encyclical alienated bishops from their pastors and pastors from their flocks. The NFPC used many of its scarce resources to provide support to Washington, D.C., priests who had been suspended by Cardinal Patrick O'Boyle for criticizing the encyclical. Bernardin, a loyal churchman, supported the encyclical but did all that he could to ease the pain of the quarrel which saw priestly departures, the resignation of one promising bishop, and faculty dismissals from Catholic University of America.

He served in the general secretary's position until 1972, helping to restructure the organization and to add the United States Catholic Conference (USCC), the administrative arm of the NCCB.

The general secretary operates from an eagle's nest. Little that happens in the American church escapes his attention. Bernardin had a unique opportunity to observe the episcopal openings and to spot the talent coming through the ranks. During these years he became a confidant of hundreds of bishops, a man almost famous for his prudence and discretion. One observer marveled that he kept so many confidences that he wondered "how Joe could sort them all out." He also was in a position to advise the apostolic delegate, Archbishop Jean Jadot, on the appointment of more pastoral American bishops.

During his term as general secretary, Bernardin undertook a massive, in-depth study of the priesthood. The psychological aspects were studied by Eugene Kennedy, the aforementioned biographer, then a professor of psychology at Loyola University of Chicago. Andrew M. Greeley, priest sociologist, examined the sociology of priesthood. Now, nearly thirty years later, some

priests claim that it was the best study every done, but the nervous bishops did not appear anxious to learn — or reveal — that
much about themselves. The project caused a great deal of con-
troversy, and Bernardin had to struggle to maintain the delicate
balance.

During these years, too, Bernardin used his considerable influence to restructure the conference, making it more representative
and responsive. Its administrative arm, the USCC, made it possible for lower clergy and laity to be part of the machinery of
government.

The future cardinal wanted to involve priests and laity in the
conference, but, in the years that followed the restructuring, there
were efforts not only to limit the conference to the bishops only
but also to do away with it entirely. At the Vatican, some curial
leaders were threatened by national conferences. Until literally
hours before he died, Bernardin was trying to hold the structure
together.

✠

In 1972 Joseph Bernardin was named archbishop of Cincinnati. He inherited an archdiocese of some 230 parishes and
540,000 Catholics. He predecessors included some old-school
triumphalists who led princely lives.

Bernardin moved from the episcopal mansion to the seminary
and a small suite. He also undertook a strenuous diet, losing fifty
pounds, bringing his considerable weight to well under two hundred pounds and, unlike many other dieters, keeping it off for
the remainder of his life. During a dinner visit, I asked him how
he kept his weight off, in spite of a genuine passion for good
food. "Will power," he answered. I could have killed him.

In 1974 Bernardin was elected to a three-year term as president of the NCCB/USCC, a position he held until 1977. During
this time, the 1976 presidential election was held, pitting Jimmy

Carter against Gerald Ford. According to Tom Fox, author of *Sexuality and Catholicism* and editor of the lay-edited *National Catholic Reporter,* "Gerald Ford agreed with the bishops on abortion and little else; Jimmy Carter agreed with them on a series of issues, but disagreed with them on abortion." The differing viewpoints set up a polarity that has yet to be resolved. Republicans appeared to be pro-life, while taking a hard, negative stand on many social issues — from capital punishment to the needs of welfare children. The Democrats were viewed as pro-choice but with a much richer social conscience. While diocesan newspapers filled pages with anti-abortion rhetoric, other issues often received only perfunctory treatment. For Bernardin, a strong supporter of pro-life issues, it was a painful dilemma. Speaking for the NCCB, Bernardin called the Democratic party's platform "irresponsible" even as the Republicans called for a constitutional amendment to outlaw abortions. The dispute led to the impression that the bishops supported a Republican ticket, something Bernardin regretted.

Carter won the presidential election. Although he lasted only one term, the impression that the bishops supported a Republican ticket lasted into the 1990s.

By 1983, Bernardin had succeeded to Chicago and had been made a cardinal. Before his installation he urged friends to remain at home and to give the travel money to useful causes. Prior to that, newly minted cardinals were known to fill chartered planes for such occasions, often creating pressure on would-be admirers.

In 1983, with his fellow bishops, he released the pastoral letter, *The Challenge of Peace: God's Promise and Our Response.* The pastoral was Bernardin's best effort. It was 45,000 words long — too long according to some critics. Yet it was vintage Bernardin. It grew because he strove for consensus. He wanted to include the sentiments of other bishops who had taken the time to study the document. According to Tom Fox, the "peace pastoral," as it was often referred to, "offered a conditional approval of the American nuclear arsenal and called for a bilateral halt in the development and deployment of new nuclear weapons." Bernardin would later amend his position to call for a complete ban on nuclear weapons.

The pastoral would upset the Reagan administration, which was larded with conservative Catholics. Even before it was released, Reagan administrators had issued a sharp seven-page criticism of the document, without sending a copy to Bernardin.

The document, however, started a dialogue. It changed the way in which bishops would interact with government. Bishops were no longer invited to the White House to serve as wallpaper. They were moral leaders who deserved to be heard.

John Paul II may have had reservations himself about the peace document. "I never lived under Communism," Bernardin would say some years later. "I don't know what it was like." But, in a private audience with Bernardin, the pope gave his approval. Years later, his encyclicals, *Veritatis Splendor* and *Evangelium Vitae* would contain trace elements of *The Challenge of Peace,* a discovery that would please Bernardin immensely. The pope's words were an implicit endorsement of his "consistent ethic of life."

✛

In December 1983, just over a year following his appointment, Bernardin traveled to Fordham University in New York, where he introduced the concept of the consistent ethic of life. During the question-and-answer period that followed his talk, he used the expression "seamless garment," a metaphor that captured the imagination of millions of American Catholics, including at least twenty-three bishops who were members of Pax Christi, a national organization dedicated to peace issues.

The seamless garment metaphor remains not fully developed

but, basically, it holds that all life is sacred. It deals with ecological issues, spousal and sexual abuse, mercy killing, capital punishment — all the issues concerning life. Under Bernardin's guidelines, abortion could no longer stand alone. It had to be understood within the context of all life.

The consistent ethic issue caused problems for him, especially from his fellow bishops, some of whom felt that support for the elimination of capital punishment would soften their stand on abortion. While cardinals such as Bernard Law of Boston and John O'Connor of New York were viewed as "single issue" bishops, Bernardin of Chicago was characterized as soft on abortion and weak-kneed on capital crime. Bernardin continued, however, to hold that human life is both sacred and social. "Because we esteem human life as sacred," he explained, "we have a duty to protect and foster it at all stages of development from conception to natural death and in all circumstances. Because we acknowledge that human life is also social, society must protect and foster it."

Even as he lay dying, he sent an appeal to the United States Supreme Court, urging it not to find that terminally ill people have a constitutional right to doctor-assisted suicide. "I am at the end of my earthly life," Bernardin wrote. "There is much that I have contemplated these last few months of my illness, but as one who is dying, I have especially come to appreciate the gift of life."

The timing was particularly ironic. On the very day that Bernardin announced that his cancer was terminal, Dr. Jack Kevorkian, the "suicide doctor," presided at his thirty-ninth assisted suicide — that of a man with pancreatic cancer.

In his three-hundred-word letter, which was sent to the court by the Catholic Health Association, Bernardin wrote that the issue was an important public matter, not simply a private decision between patient and doctor. "Our legal and ethical tradition has held consistently that suicide, assisted suicide, and euthanasia are wrong because they involve a direct attack on innocent life."

Bernardin understood the difference between the dying person who decides to forgo treatment and one who chooses death. But he drew a distinction between such a decision by a patient and one by a court of law.

✠

Nationally, even during his years with the NCCB/USCCC, few bishops have been called upon more than Bernardin for help with internal problems. His habits of consensus building and patience are legendary. In one high-profile case dating to 1983, the archbishop of Seattle, Raymond Hunthausen, together with the two other bishops of Washington State had published a statement titled *Prejudice against Homosexuals and the Ministry of the Church* in which they suggested a "rethinking and development" of the issue. Archbishop Hunthausen also welcomed Dignity, an organization of some five thousand Catholic gays and lesbians, to celebrate its biannual convention Mass in Seattle's St. James Cathedral. Hunthausen immediately came under attack and was eventually supplied with an unwanted auxiliary bishop, Donald Wuerl, now bishop of Pittsburgh, who would take over many of his duties.

When the liberal protests grew louder than the conservatives who had protested against Hunthausen, Bernardin, together with Cardinal O'Connor of New York and Archbishop John Quinn of San Francisco, was asked to mediate the matter. While the prudent cardinal refused to discuss the details, he told me that he had spent eight hours on a single day attempting to find a solution. Eventually, a consensus was reached. Thomas J. Murphy, bishop of Great Falls–Billings, Montana, was named coadjutor archbishop. Donald Wuerl returned to his native Pittsburgh, where he was named bishop in 1988. Raymond Hunthausen retired in 1991. (Ironically, both Murphy, a Chicago native, and Wuerl are being touted as Bernardin's successor.)

✠

At the archdiocesan level, Chicago's twelfth bishop, seventh archbishop, and fifth cardinal inherited an archdiocese in terrible pain. After seventeen years of erratic rule by John Patrick Cody, the archdiocese was in chaotic condition both physically and emotionally. In fairness we must say that many of the ailments of the archdiocese were shared by the wider church. Most notably, Chicago was severely hobbled by the loss of over three hundred priests through resignations and the paucity of new vocations to replace them. There were population shifts that witnessed major parishes reduced from a dozen SRO Masses on Sunday to a single Sunday Mass attended by a few hundred people. Nationally, Mass attendance, once nearly 60 percent, had dwindled to some 25 percent.

Bernardin had to restore the morale of a dispirited clergy corps. In a memorable ceremony soon after his installation, he addressed his fellow priests. "I am your brother Joseph" he said. It was a statement that would be used again and again during his Chicago years. It captured the imagination much like "seamless garment" would do.

A similar liturgy was held in early October just before his death. It drew eight hundred priests, many in tears. The "Brother Joseph" mantra was repeated to cheering priests. Fr. Jeremiah Boland, executive secretary of the Priests Placement Board, would say after his funeral that such actions would fill the Chicago church with the spirit of possibility.

— FOUR —

Bishop as Teacher: The Bernardin Legacy

"**W**HEN HE SPOKE AND WROTE, it was about life, with all of its glorious promise and all of its ugly problems," Charles Madigan wrote of Joseph Bernardin in the *Chicago Tribune*. "He walked calmly and with determination through the moral and philosophical minefields of his age — war and peace, living and dying, the agony of problem priests, abortion, capital punishment."

Bernardin's speaking and writing followed his life itself — loving, consistent, dependable. But his words also showed vision and leadership. "The scale and horror of modern warfare, whether nuclear or not, make it totally unacceptable," he wrote long before others copied him. He wrote this at a time when nations were still hoarding nuclear weapons in case the good-guy nations needed to respond. Bernardin believed that "an eye for an eye" produced only blind people.

His words had impact. President Reagan, who had invited other bishops to the White House but not Bernardin, continued to talk tough against the Soviet Union, but gradually became an advocate of arms control.

In March 1994 Bernardin voiced strong views on health care during an address at the National Press Club in Washington, D.C. "Health care is an essential safeguard of human life and dignity, and there is an obligation for society to ensure that every person be able to realize this right," he told the reporters. The speech influenced Bill Clinton's efforts to push a national health care bill through the Congress. The bill didn't make it through the Congress, but Clinton has pledged to try again.

✠

His writing consumed him. He believed in the power of words. Two weeks before he died, he reviewed the contents of a speech he had been working on for several months with one of his auxiliary bishops, George V. Murry, S.J. "The Importance of Ethics and Values in Our Fast-Changing World" was read by Murry at Elmhurst College because the cardinal was too ill to attend.

In the address Bernardin cited a litany of developments, including advances in medical and computer technology and the end of the Cold War, that have complicated modern life. These complications, he wrote, have been amplified by moral vacillation by individuals and political and economic institutions. He called for a response, not only from individuals but also corporations and politicians as well. "In the testimony and example of people of good will, others will find motivation to respond to their own inner urgings to rise above isolation and the resulting lack of meaning in their lives," he wrote. "Just as important, the institutions that we represent must also give credible witness to these values — by our corporate policies, by our own sense of meaning and experience of community."

The self-effacing cardinal would often preface his writings or remarks by insisting, "I am not a theologian." But such self-deprecation belied a long career of writing that has had a marked impact on modern religious and ethical thought. He covered issues ranging from abortion to nuclear proliferation and was regarded as a genuine thinker among the American Catholic hierarchy. Typically, his "consistent ethic of life" teachings expanded the framework of discussion from abortion through capital punishment and leading into health care, spousal abuse, and ecology. Although his words could be labored at times because of his compulsive need to nuance each phrase, he had an ability to bring people together in a relatively peaceful atmosphere so that they could not only talk but listen to each other.

✠

Since the end of the second century, bishops have exercised three principal functions: teaching, leading, and sanctifying. Bishops may have been even more important in those early days. They generally remained in their dioceses for life and were so revered that, if they could not preside, a portion of Eucharistic bread consecrated by them was generally placed in the local pastor's chalice.

Cardinal Bernardin took his teaching role seriously. Further, the former high school teacher genuinely enjoyed teaching, even though it involved a measure of risk. Prudent bishops do not write. Unless they echo the sentiments of a papal letter, they could run the risk of Vatican scrutiny. Further, John Paul II has been a prolific writer, turning out a dozen encyclicals in his first years in office, as well as countless shorter papers and allocutions on a wide range of issues. In comparison Paul VI reigned sixteen years and turned out only five encyclicals.

More docile bishops are intimidated. Most limit themselves to treatises on the Blessed Mother, appeals for vocations, and condemnations of abortion — all safe topics. "Rome loves docile and careerist bishops," one auxiliary bishop observed. "They don't respect them, but they know they'll do anything the Vatican wants."

Cardinal Bernardin's writings could withstand the most careful scrutiny. However, just the fact that he wrote could make him suspect. An earlier cardinal, John Henry Newman (1801–90), one of the great Catholic thinkers of the nineteenth century, a man largely responsible for the renewal of interest in the writings of the Fathers of the Church and for a deeper appreciation of the role of the laity in the development of doctrine, left a deposit of some fifteen thousand documents. His cause for canonization has been slowed dramatically by cautious scholars who scrutinize his words for any hint of deviant thinking.

In his recent study, *Inside the Vatican,* Jesuit scholar Thomas J. Reese acknowledges that he was especially grateful to the many cardinals and bishops he interviewed both in Rome and the U.S., but reported that most wanted to remain anonymous. "This in itself says much about politics in the Vatican," Reese observed.

Yet, the monarchial system that creates bishops causes them to be quickly forgotten following their deaths unless they leave a body of writings after them. It's difficult to predict just how much Bernardin's prolific output will outlive him. However, Tom Fox, editor of the *National Catholic Reporter,* has cited Bernardin often in his editorials and books. He believes that his legacy will bring the cardinal to the status of prophet.

"Here, you've seen this before," the cardinal said to me during an interview in 1990. "It's my pastoral letter on the church [*The Family Gathered Here before You*]. "My first pastoral was on liturgy, particularly the Sunday Eucharist," he continued, as we discussed his writings. "I agree that bishops should write their own pastorals, but there is also a place for collective pastorals, like the ones being published by the bishops' conference." (The Vatican, some bishops, and a small but vocal group of conservatives object not only to collective pastorals but also to the national conferences themselves, especially the NCCB.) He was disappointed by the modest attention his pastoral on the church had received. It was released just before he had announced the closings and consolidations of more than three dozen parishes and the attention had shifted.

The cardinal appeared always caught between a rock and a hard place. Just when something such as a positive pastoral was to be released, the specter of closing or merging dozens of parishes would take precedence in the religious news. Instead of excerpts from a pastoral he had polished for upward of two years, the papers had to cover pickets at the Pastoral Center.

Also, in common with other bishops, he was constantly dealing with Vatican bureaucrats who had a facility for watering sparks. It could often take four or five letters to get a single decision from the Vatican, often regarding matters that should have been handled at the local level. The principle of subsidiarity, that decisions should be made at the lowest possible level, did not take root in the Vatican.

Chicago has much in common with the diocese of Rome, over which the pope presides as bishop of Rome. Rome has about 200,000 more Catholics but only 330 parishes, nearly 50 less than Chicago. Mass attendance, particularly in the city of Rome is quite low compared with Chicago. Yet the diocese has some 950 priests, not counting hundreds of resident priests who are working in the Vatican or studying in Rome. It simply doesn't feel the priest shortage in the same way. Its churches often have only one Mass on Sunday, while Chicago generally has at least three in each church. Rome is presided over by two cardinals, two archbishops, six bishops, and a staff of 150, even as Bernardin sometimes waited over a year for an auxiliary. Further, Bernardin had to deal with finger-wagging cautions about American laxity. Yet, according to Thomas J. Reese's study, 70 percent of Romans condone birth control, divorce, cohabitation, and premarital sex. While Bernardin got cautionary letters about female servers, John Paul II was visiting churches in his own diocese that used female servers well before their introduction was approved. The pope simply ignored the "abuse" but Bernardin lost precious time attempting to respond to Rome and to his local critics. Rome, it seems, views such rules as

ideals to be achieved while Americans tend to see directives as
mandatory.

John Paul II takes his duties as bishop of Rome quite seriously. He regularly confronts city officials on inadequate housing,
lack of essential services for the poor, the elderly, and the hand-
icapped, as well as AIDS victims, the mentally ill, drug addicts,
and juvenile delinquents. When Bernardin addressed these topics, he could count on being accused of sticking the church's nose
into politics, being soft on crime, or accepting of homosexual life
styles.

✠

On occasion, he was asked to comment on another bishop's
pastoral. Typically, when his neighboring archbishop, Rembert
Weakland, O.S.B. of Milwaukee, wrote a pastoral in which he
raised questions about the possibility of ordaining married men
as priests, both the *Chicago Tribune* and the *Chicago Sun-Times*
asked Bernardin to make a statement.

Bernardin liked Weakland. When the former Benedictine ab-
bot general was invited to speak in Chicago, he was always
welcomed, even at Holy Name Cathedral. But the cardinal
wasn't always happy to be drawn into no-win situations that did
nothing more than to give the appearance that he differed with
present disciplines. Thus, he answered the Weakland proposal by
first praising Weakland's commitment to the church and his candor. "Archbishop Weakland deeply loves the church," he wrote.
"He appreciates its theological and historical tradition. I see no
defiance or disregard of this tradition. Even his current proposal
regarding the ordination of married men, while certainly raising
a challenge, was made with the acknowledgment that it would
require the approval of the Holy Father."

Note the diplomatic tactic. Having gently pulled his brother
bishop away from critical gunsights and assuring all that Weak-

land is a loyal bishop, Bernardin now presents his view: "Now, personally, I hold a different view. I maintain that we have not adequately explored the possibilities of attracting men to the priesthood. If the priesthood was presented in a more positive and persuasive way, and if it were supported by the entire Catholic community, many more candidates would come forward. But I acknowledge the value of discussion that would force us to probe more deeply and to articulate more clearly our convictions in this matter," he continued. "I stand with the church. I've taken an oath to uphold the church's teaching and discipline. I work within the parameters that have been set by the church." This was a classic Bernardin response. Honey, not vinegar.

His efforts to improve the vocation pool were less than successful. At times, he had upward of eight people working in the Office of Vocations, but the ordination numbers remained abysmally low, although millions were spent on the seminary system. It was an issue that bewildered him somewhat. He loved the priesthood.

Although he could get depressed, his morale was always healthy. He died believing that the vocation situation would improve and, perhaps more important, that it could not be improved by clamping down. "I instinctively believe that it's healthier to let people say what they want. Let them get whatever it is out of their system."

As archbishop of Cincinnati, he wrote four pastorals dealing with the education of children, prayer, priesthood, and preaching. During his Chicago years, he issued five letters. They dealt with liturgy, Jesus and his meaning for Christian life, ministry, the church, and health care. He also wrote a weekly column for the *New World*, the archdiocesan newspaper.

In addition there were eight letters classed as "guidelines." They covered a broad range: the disabled, religious life, two on religious education (one concerning children, another for adults), AIDS, charismatic renewal, parish life in a contemporary church, and the permanent diaconate. (With 587 deacons, the Chicago church has the largest corps in the U.S. church. He wrote this letter to acknowledge the twenty-fifth year of the diaconate.) His final guidelines were issued in May 1996. They addressed parish sharing.

In November 1994 he set a precedent by hosting a video pastoral. It was aimed at youth and titled *Here and Now*. He appeared relaxed during this presentation. TV seemed to excite him and cause him to be more spontaneous. Somehow, in spite of growing difficulties of finances and adequate personnel, he seemed to have settled in. His normal speaking style resembled his writings: cautious, reserved, carefully phrased. In this video he was more animated.

In 1995 he embarked on a new pastoral letter on liturgy. It was based on reports from working groups that had evaluated the status of the liturgical celebration in his diocese. Several crews were working on a video to accompany his pastoral letter. The video was intended to show examples of model liturgies and was to be narrated by Bernardin. But the project, just three weeks from completion, had to be set aside as he neared death.

✠

"I seem to be at the focal point when the press and others want reactions," he told me during our longest interview. "When I speak, even if I make it clear that I am speaking personally or that I am expressing an opinion, it is usually viewed as the authoritative statement of a bishop and a cardinal. People interpret everything I say in the light of who I am."

Bernardin's priest corps genuinely liked him. "He's the best that's out there," the more cynical ones would say. Others gave him high marks, although they sometimes grew impatient about the flow of often tedious paperwork and the necessity of putting proposals through layers of bureaucracy. Critics sometimes felt that the core administration imitated the worst faults of the business world.

In spite of his reasoned writings, Bernardin was not always obeyed. "The only power the church has is the power we give it," Marquette University theologian Daniel Maguire wrote. It became even more true of a gentle bishop such as Bernardin because he was most reluctant to issue decrees wrapped in punitive threats.

Politically, Bernardin got embroiled in a dispute with Richard Phelan, a devout Catholic and successful trial lawyer, who had been elected president of the Cook County Board, the most populated county in Illinois and the one that embraces Chicago. During his campaign, Phelan promised to reinstate abortions at Cook County Hospital. Bernardin had written and spoken often on the subject. For two years, both in private and in public, the two leaders had differed. By 1992, Phelan issued the order to restore abortions at the hospital. The cardinal understood Phelan's position but he was hurt.

During a polite quarrel with his priests regarding general absolution, Bernardin had little choice but to point to his published guidelines. But the issue brought to the front the role of pastors in making pastoral decisions. They believed that their discretion should not only cover the practice of general absolution but also certain cases involving marriage, baptisms, annulments, and church burial. Some pastors sincerely believed that the grid of canon law simply did not fit over the lived experiences of many of their parishioners. Parishioners arrived at the rectory door with stories of marriages they hardly remembered, let alone could validate or invalidate. "I just have to take them at the front door," one pastor said, "and tell them to leave their sins behind."

"I feel caught in the middle between the magisterium to which I belong and am bound to support," the cardinal said, "and the pastors and their people to whom I am obligated to listen and to be a good shepherd." Bernardin's ongoing dialogue with both priests and people did not always find a common ground. Occasionally, he discovered that he had to write one guideline while tolerating another.

F. Scott Appleby, director of the Cushwa Center for the Study of American Catholicism at the University of Notre Dame, observed in a *Chicago Tribune* interview that even if Bernardin did not find common ground in every instance, his style was one the church will need in years to come.

"You persuade people when you've listened to them long enough to understand what kind of appeal will strike a chord," Appleby told the *Tribune*. "Bernardin helped move the church away from the notion that here is the church teaching its doctrine and the people passively accepting."

The cardinal's style was more reminiscent of an earlier church where local communities were highly autonomous, often electing their own bishops and following their own customs. Gradually, however, Fr. Reese records that a practice developed of notifying Rome when a new bishop was elected because these communities wanted to be in communion with the church of Rome. This led to the need for Roman approval and finally Roman appointment of these men. Uniformity was also assured by mandating uniform practices in liturgy, church law, and seminary training. Doctrinal unity was encouraged through papal writings and the swift suppression of dissent.

✠

In recent years Vatican control has reached ludicrous proportions. The November 1996 meeting of the National Conference of Catholic Bishops witnessed grown men quibbling about the use of the word "priest" versus "presbyter." Sadder still were the words of one conservative archbishop: "Don't worry. It's not over yet. Rome must approve. They'll come our way."

The situation has caused acerbic writers such as Andrew Greeley, a priest of the Chicago church, sociologist, and novelist, to make grim predictions about the cardinal's successor. In Greeley's opinion the Vatican sees the Chicago church as "a mess, created by a good man who was far too permissive. A strong man must be sent to clean up the mess," Greeley continued. "He must give orders, make rules, and enforce them." Greeley sees the successor as "narrow, rigid, insensitive, authoritarian, probably incompetent, and utterly incapable of listening."

Another prolific writer, Fr. Richard McBrien, a member of the theology department at the University of Notre Dame, wrote that "Chicago will probably have to wait a very long time before it has a real successor to Joseph Bernardin. He will have to be a whole and holy human being, utterly committed to the gospel of Jesus Christ, completely honest with himself and others, and with a thoroughly pastoral heart. This profile has often been ignored in appointing bishops over the past eighteen years. "A replacement for Bernardin, yes," McBrien continued. "But a successor will take longer."

— FIVE —

Stories of Grace

"WHEN YOU'RE NOT CERTAIN what a person is thinking," a psychologist friend once said to me, "watch what they're doing." The insightful axiom applied to Joseph Bernardin. Although following his death innumerable friends, while reflecting on his life, insisted that the private Bernardin was no different than the public one, the fact is that he could often be a genuine enigma.

One respected television interviewer reported that he had interviewed the cardinal not long after he arrived in Chicago. "I dug and dug," he said. "I couldn't get a thing out of him." The "open" cardinal could be as tight as the top olive in a bottle.

"He was a a a real enigma," an investigative reporter said of him. "He answered my questions, but I wasn't always certain what he was really thinking."

Part of the mystery can be traced to a character trait of his father who, Bernardin recalled, was exceptionally prudent. The cardinal would often polish a sentence until it was so vague that it seemed to mask his full intentions. His arguments could be elliptical; he could appear to say something declarative in the first half of a statement and take it back in the second half. "I cannot speak about the ordination of women," he once said to me. "If I do, I'll be accused of favoring it. But, if I don't, I will be accused of being against it. All I can do is point to existing church teaching and try to get people to accept that." (Later, this would change. Toward the end of his life, he said

81

to Sister Donna Quinn, O.P., a strong advocate for women's issues, "I personally favor the ordination of women. But this is not the time.")

Part of the ecclesiastical veil and personal reserve may have stemmed from his role as CEO of an immense corporation. The archdiocese covers an area of 1,411 square miles and includes 378 Catholic parishes, 277 Catholic elementary schools, and 3 seminaries. Catholic Charities of the archdiocese is the largest private social agency in the Midwest. It served 500,000 people in 1995 alone. Its school system is the largest parochial school system in the U.S. and the eleventh largest school system of any kind in the country.

The archdiocese employs approximately nineteen thousand people, including more diocesan priests than entire states such as Florida and Indiana. Bernardin may have reveled in this huge organization, once the second biggest corporation in the state of Illinois, but he could never forget it either. He was not unlike someone constantly on trial. Anything he said could be used against him.

The anecdotes that follow, then, are hints of an explanation into the man's real personality and character. They became especially true of him in the final years of his life when he came to realize that his train had made its last stop. The false accusations of sexual abuse made against him provided him with a second birth and the discovery of cancer freed him, making him even stronger. He found the priest within himself that had occasionally gotten lost under the watered silk.

These are stories, then, largely involving the small change of his Chicago years. Yet they define his priesthood better than anything else he did.

During his funeral rites, no one mentioned his election to seven successive synods of bishops, his chairmanship of numerous committees of the Bishops' Conference, the Catholic Church Extension Society, and Catholic University of America. Instead, people focused on his unique ability to reach people through small acts. That is what follows.

✠

Cardinal Bernardin liked to visit schools. Such visits were largely connected with celebrations of one kind or another. He could relax. One day, accompanied by Dr. Elaine Schuster, superintendent of schools, he entered a primary school classroom and squeezed himself into one of the tiny desks. When introduced as a cardinal, one student said: "I thought cardinals were birds."

Bernardin, ever the teacher, patiently explained that there were other species of cardinals. The more he attempted to explain, the deeper he got into their debt.

"Do you pray all day," one asked. "What does a cardinal do?" His need to be accurate only sunk him deeper. Finally, he turned to Schuster and said: "I think I should have just said I was a bird."

✠

In spite of his lofty status, Bernardin could often go unrecognized in public. He once told me that he had walked from his mansion to Diversey and Clark Streets — more than a mile — without being recognized. I once observed him in Marshall Field's, making a small purchase. It was clear that the clerk did not recognize him. He genuinely liked these privacies at least as much as he enjoyed being recognized.

Once, while visiting St. Mary of the Woods Parish to bless an extension to the school, he was making his way across the schoolyard with Fr. Andrew Greeley, who celebrates Sunday Mass in the parish. It was getting toward the scheduled time of the liturgy. A nervous staffer looked out and asked a young student: "Did you see the cardinal?"

"No," he answered. "All I saw was Fr. Greeley and some priest."

Other cardinals travel in retinues, emerging from stretch limousines accompanied by solemn-faced careerists who had arranged convenient — and often illegal — parking in front of the church. Some bishops write letters to parishes they will visit with detailed requests regarding a private room for vesting, a presider's chair, a directive that no female servers be present, etc. Bernardin generally arrived alone, searched for a parking spot, carried his own baggage, and vested in the sacristy with his fellow priests.

✠

Fr. John W. Calicott, pastor of Holy Angels Parish on Chicago's south side, recalled a parish visit early in Bernardin's administration which did not promise to be a pleasant one. Holy Angels is an all-black, activist parish, often at the cutting edge of social change. The parishioners were ready to challenge this white southerner on virtually every phase of the local church's treatment of African-Americans.

The Chicago church's record on race relations is not one of its proudest achievements. Its churches were closed to blacks, then opened only after the whites had abandoned them. Its schools did not admit blacks for years, and it wasn't until the 1960s that its hospitals accepted black patients. In some parishes, blacks waiting on line for confession were required to go to the end of the line with the approach of a white person. If admitted to a Catholic cemetery at all, blacks were buried by the outer wall.

Yet, in fairness, Chicago's record stands out in comparison to other dioceses, including Bernardin's home diocese of Charleston. In many dioceses, if African Americans were admitted to church at all, it was to stand in the back and receive the Eucharist from a priest other than the presider.

Against these generations of pain, emerging black Catholics

were in no mood to hear their bishop announce "the time is not opportune," as one of Bernardin's predecessors said throughout his reign.

The cardinal came to Holy Angels to listen. And he got a respectful but firm earful. Joseph Bernardin's greatest weapon may have been his ears. He could listen by the hour — absorbing, weighing, sorting out. Unlike other authority figures, he didn't feel the need to assert his power. He did not view appeals to his authority as challenges to it. He cut no one off. He would occasionally say, "May I say this?" — as if asking permission to respond.

At Holy Angels, he listened to a litany of concerns. Then he responded (given here in paraphrase): "I grew up in the South. Black people lived apart from white people. I never learned about them. There is so much that I don't know. You'll have to help me, to teach me."

Throughout his administration, he tried mightily to repair the damage of years of neglect. Yet, his hands were tied by rising costs, deteriorating buildings, shifting populations, and only slowly changing attitudes. He refused to hear recommendations that non-Catholics not be admitted to inner-city schools. "We should be there," he said. "We should be educating regardless of religious affiliation."

✠

In another black parish, St. Elizabeth's, Bernardin had come to dedicate the new church. The church, pastored by the priests and brothers of the Society of the Divine Word, a congregation well-known for its work among minorities, had just been completed. During a colorful yet reverent celebration, the cardinal stood for most of the liturgy. Near the close of the Mass, during a prolonged Kiss of Peace, I visited with him briefly at the altar. Sweat was rolling down his face; his hands were trembling.

"What's wrong?" I asked. "I'm feeling awful," he said. "I've got an kidney infection."

"Why did you come?" I asked, almost rebuking him.

"I promised," he said. "I promised them."

My path to St. Elizabeth's had been opened by my wife, Jean. As a member of the Art and Architecture Commission of the archdiocese, she had been asked to visit the "temporary" church and to make recommendations for its remodeling.

St. Elizabeth's was founded in 1881 to serve Irish Catholics. By 1924, population shifts had extended Chicago's "black belt." The parish was combined with St. Monica's, another black parish. It soon became the center of Chicago's black community, although for years the parish tolerated a dual system of education in its elementary school, one for whites, another for blacks.

In 1930 the huge church was destroyed by a fire of suspicious origin. Within a year, the parish hall had been converted into a temporary church. (Cardinal Mundelein claimed the insurance coverage, saying that "the colored have enough churches.")

Nothing was done for sixty years. After Jean visited, she recommended that nothing be done to rescue the old hall. By this time, one could clearly see through the thin walls. But she urged the building of a new church in this inner city area.

Bernardin reviewed the reports from the commission and the SVDs. Sensing a genuine need for a continued church presence in a parish located in the shadow of the Taylor Homes, a desperately poor housing project, he ordered that a new church be built. It cost over $1,000,000. Fundraising efforts realized only a fraction of this amount. The archdiocese paid the balance.

The cardinal had told me often that he could not repair all the injustices of the past, but he would try. When a young, untested black architect was selected, he immediately approved him over established and clout-heavy white architects.

The new church thrives today, an island of beauty and peace. It has been a beacon, actually helping to lower crime in the area.

✠

The racial/poor stories continue. Not long after Bernardin
was named archbishop, Sister Margaret Traxler, S.S.N.D., approached him and told him of her desire to open a shelter for
homeless women and their children on Chicago's southwest side.
St. Carthage Parish, once an Irish bastion, had closed its doors
in the early 1980s. Traxler saw the property as an ideal place to
open the Maria Shelter, a facility that would accept homeless
women and their children. She had little funding and Bernardin
was under pressure from some of his advisors to get maximum
income through the sale or rental of the property. Further, Sister
Margaret was seen as a troublesome rebel by many of the more
cautious clerics. In fact, she could be classed as a heretic, since
she openly opposed the church's teaching on birth control and
was pro-choice on abortion. Clearly, the official church could
not support her shelter while it was still linked to the official
structure.

Bernardin listened. One could speak to him and not to the
authority he was supposed to represent.

He turned the entire property over to her for one dollar.

Later, in 1992, Traxler found an unused convent not far from
Maria Shelter. "I begged the cardinal for it," she told me. "You
don't have to beg in order to do God's work," he told her. He
gave her the convent. It is now a temporary home for over
twenty working women.

✠

During his administration, Bernardin had to deal constantly with
the politics of cutback. He had to close over eighty parishes,
merging most of them with others. He closed or merged over
a hundred schools, including a popular seminary high school on
the city's south side.

Quigley South Seminary High School had been built in 1960 to relieve the overcrowding at the original Quigley High School on Chicago's near north side. By the time it was dedicated in 1962, it had 869 students. Like its older brother, Quigley South was a four-year high school where potential priests were encouraged to test their vocation. Dropout rates were always high. In the best of years, the school sent only about thirty graduates to the college level of seminary training.

In the years that followed costs rose dramatically even as numbers declined. Nationally, less than ten seminary high schools, enrolling under a thousand students, had survived. Yet the school had created fierce loyalties. Some observers claimed that the non-priest alumni of the two Quigleys were more loyal than the ordained grads.

Something else had happened. The neighborhood east of Quigley South was becoming increasingly black. The quality school with its attractive subsidized tuition became an elite prep school for many African American boys.

The closing was poorly handled. Even as students and their families were being assured by the principal that the school would not close, archdiocesan planners were planning its closing. Finally, abruptly, the announcement was made that the school would close.

Pastors, parents, students, and alumni were furious. An after-the-fact meeting held at the school was marked by shouting and accusations. The cries of the people did not penetrate the sound-proof walls of administrative infallibility. "The school will close when His Eminence says it will close!" one tense official shouted.

Bernardin backed his staff. But some of his pastors rebelled. Fr. Michael Pfleger, pastor of St. Sabina's, a nearly all-black parish, led a group of high school seminarians in a sit-in at the Pastoral Center. An archdiocesan official pointed to Pfleger and announced: "We'll get you for this!"

Fr. Michael Ivers, pastor of St. Agatha's, an all-black parish, called the decision — and Bernardin — a racist. It would be years before the chancery office regained a measure of respect, but it took the removal of a number of administrators.

After the smoke cleared, things settled down. The wounds have never quite healed. Most of its high school seminarians did not transfer to the other high school seminary. Some left the church entirely.

When Cardinal Bernardin met Fr. Ivers sometime after the bitter closing, he didn't chide him or attempt to "get him." Instead, he asked simply: "Mike, how can I regain your trust and respect?" It was pure Bernardin. Unlike many people in high positions, he knew how to say he was sorry.

✠

One evening the cardinal and a female staff member visited a church institution to help settle a serious quarrel. When the door opened, the spokesperson for the group said: "He gets in. She doesn't."

The cardinal asked them to close the door. He stood outside with his aide and asked: "Carol, which fight do we want to make?"

She agreed and waited in the car. When he emerged, he said: "Well, we made some progress."

Purists would insist that he should have walked away. But consensus building is a game of inches. He would return to the other issue at another time.

✠

Before the Vatican reluctantly gave permission for females to serve as acolytes, the majority of Chicago churches were already using them. When Bernardin issued an announcement that they were still not officially sanctioned, Sister Donna Quinn, O.P.,

leader of Chicago Catholic Women, organized a group of grandparents to call the cardinal. The grandparents were adults, no
longer willing to accept truths as if handed down from on high.
Bernardin got the message. He issued no mandates and quietly
let the thoroughly innocent practice continue while other bishops
hurled thunderbolts.

✠

Perhaps the most unsettling quarrel during his Chicago years was
with the gay and lesbian community. It was never quite settled.
Yet more than a week before his death, details were quietly arranged to have the Windy City Gay Chorus sing two ten-minute
sets during the wake.

Given the shaky relationship with the church, the chorus decided to put the invitation to a vote. Nearly percent of the
eighty-five-member group accepted. In several major cities, including San Francisco, New York, and Boston, gay choruses are
expressly prohibited from performing on church property.

It was an issue that plagued his administration, bringing criticism from both sides. He wanted to minister to gays but an Ice
Age Vatican administration had blocked every effort. His critics believed that his outreach went too far. But for Bernardin
spiritual benefits outweighed political risks.

From 1970 until 1986, dioceses tolerated a Catholic group
named Dignity which held religious services within the churches.
The national organization had been founded by an Augustinian
priest in San Diego in 1969. Word of mouth has fueled its
growth. In Chicago they now meet on Sunday evenings with a
eucharistic liturgy at a local Methodist church.

In 1986 the now famous Ratzinger letter of "clarification"
termed homosexuality "an objective disorder" and "a more or less
strong tendency toward an intrinsic moral evil." Around the U.S.
local bishops reacted by banning Dignity from the church.

Bernardin reacted much as his fellow bishops, but with a difference. Two weeks after the Ratzinger letter, he met privately with the leaders of Dignity. When he was informed that gays had grown up in the church hating themselves, he urged them not to.

In 1988 he organized the Archdiocesan Gay and Lesbian Organization (AGLO). The group doesn't officially challenge church teaching on gay relationships. It draws some two hundred people each Sunday night at Our Lady of Mount Carmel Church on Chicago's north side. Again, while other bishops were banning gay groups, forbidding nuns and priests from ministering to them and virtually ignoring the AIDS crisis, Chicago Catholic gays had found a home. Initially, there was great tension between Dignity and AGLO. Now the two groups have settled their quarrel. Bernardin himself has presided at two AGLO liturgies since 1988. In addition he donated $200,000 and an unused convent to what became Bonaventure House, a residence for thirty people living with AIDS.

✠

Writers attract all kinds of letters, including some from people who vastly overestimate our influence. I received one some years ago. It had to do with a former priest who was dying of AIDS. Given the low regard in which AIDS victims, especially clergy, were held, I could understand that a man could be dying without benefit of clergy.

He had returned to Chicago to be near his mother. He was a patient in a non-sectarian hospital, one of only three that would accept AIDS patients at that time.

He got word to me that he wanted a priest to usher him into eternity. Asked which one he wanted, he named a priest who had left the ministry some years before. The man was contacted and agreed to come. He also asked for a gay priest, and a good man from a religious order was contacted.

Later, I told the cardinal the sad story. He listened and then said, "I know. I was there."

Someone had contacted him. He went alone, but not unidentified, to the north side hospital. It was during the early years of the AIDS crisis and the majority of people were terrified of the AIDS contagion. Bernardin shared the same fears, but visited with the dying priest.

✝

The Chicago church has lost an estimated three hundred priests through resignations since the great exodus began in the 1960s. Most have remained as faithful to the church as they were when working in parishes. Yet, sadly, they are often treated badly. "We are dead men," one said. "They speak of us as if we were dead."

Not so with Bernardin. Not long after he arrived in Chicago, a group of resigned priests invited him to join them for an evening. For years, they called their little prayer group "The Upper Room." They gathered regularly to share Scripture, insights, and prayer.

Bernardin accepted. The surprised group met to discuss the format of the evening. Then they decided simply to follow the format of their regular meetings. If the cardinal wanted to speak he could wait his turn and speak just as they did.

He did just that. When he spoke, he thanked them for their service and confided that he had thought of resigning from time to time. "Somehow, however, I never did," he said without a trace of rebuke toward them. He paid particular tribute to their wives. There wasn't a hint of the "that woman" syndrome that so infects some frightened bishops.

Some time later a group of them, led by Marty Hegarty, founder of a group called WEORC, which counsels men and women who are leaving the priesthood or religious life, approached him and suggested that those who had served twenty years or more and who reached the age of seventy should be given a pension, just as diocesan priests were. He agreed. "It was a question of simple justice," he told me later.

He helped the group to develop a list of qualified recipients, some of whom genuinely needed the modest pension. An estimated thirty-five resigned and over-seventy priests now receive a well-deserved monthly check.

✠

Bernardin loved the media and used it effectively. "He never met a microphone he didn't like," his friend Msgr. Ken Velo declared.

Following his death, four of us were asked to be on a public television panel in order to discuss his influence. All four of us were cradle Catholics, but the vaccination had taken in various ways. We were all supposed to be objective, at arm's length distance from the man we all liked.

Under persistent and intelligent questioning by Joel Weismann, a lawyer and host of *Chicago Week in Review,* we all agreed that we had been manipulated by the archbishop in one way or another. Yet none of us minded. The cardinal had used a rare technique to manipulate the media: he told the truth.

At one conference, not long before he entered his final illness, Andrew Herrmann, religion writer for the *Chicago Sun-Times,* was pressing Bernardin persistently for some hint about his successor. Herrmann later recalled that the cardinal had "glared at him with those slate eyes." His answers were short and sharp. And he gave away nothing.

Following the conference, Bernardin grabbed Herrmann's crossed arms. "Andrew, I'm sorry I couldn't answer your questions," he whispered. "Cardinal," Herrmann answered, "I'm sorry I had to ask them."

A radio reporter overheard the exchange and yelled: "Hey, it's a fight!" Bernardin turned and said: "Oh, no. Andrew and I are old friends." Later, he would write Herrmann and thank him for giving up a holiday weekend to cover his many appearances.

✠

Bishops often adhere to what Jesuit theologian David G. Schultenover calls the "Mediterranean model." Its principal support is "belongingness" and its primary social structure is the family (read church). "A person's identity depends on belonging to and being accepted by the family," Schultenover writes. "But that belonging and acceptance depends on one's adherence to the traditional rules of organization and maintenance."

The traditional codes are simple: honor and shame. A man's very identity hinges upon his upholding his honor. Shame falls upon whoever is responsible for maintaining order and fails to do so. It occurs whenever anyone disrupts or even criticizes the system. In such a system subordinates are always a threat to superordinates because they might bring shame. To lose control is to be shamed.

Good will, trust, and love have very little place in the Mediterranean model. Efforts at reform are read as revolts. Anyone who would call for change is routinely sent a cautionary letter that uses the word "scandal" at least once.

In such a system it is rarely the offense that matters; it is the impact on the bishop. Clergy brought on the carpet routinely report that their bishop will plead: "Do you realize what you're doing to me?" Individual consciences have little play; it is the collective conscience that rules.

Bernardin spent many years trapped within the Mediterranean model. By his own admission, he often said that he chose the institution over the individual on many occasions. In his later years, however, he became more confident in himself. Indeed, he often sounded like Bishop Jacques Gaillot of Evreaux, France, who was removed from office for having views at variance with Rome. "The score (Gospel) is wonderful," Gaillot wrote, "but the orchestra (church) plays off-key."

Some years ago, I was asked to do a series of profiles for the *New World*, the archdiocesan paper. Among them was a successful young priest who pastored two inner-city parishes. He was also elected as one of the two deans in his vicariate, a tribute to the respect in which he was held.

The pastor had introduced group reconciliation, just as many other pastors had. The Vatican, ignoring the fact that in-person confession had virtually been abandoned, condemned the practice. But in this man's parish, as in others, it had actually increased in-person confession.

I mentioned this fact parenthetically — and innocently — in my profile. Somehow, it got by the editors but not by a sharp-eyed chancery official who enjoyed playing cop. Memos were passed, and the pastor was invited for a talk with the cardinal.

"You're a pastor and a dean, Bill," the cardinal said. "Now, you're in my archdiocesan paper, admitting to an outlawed practice."

"I guess I am, Joe," the pastor answered. "I made a pastoral decision. It's working well. I'm going to keep it up."

At that point, Bernardin could have crushed him. But it wasn't his style. He liked Bill and respected his pastoral conscience.

"Well, Bill, I guess all I can say is that I talked with you," he said.

"Yep, Joe," he answered, "and all I can tell my people is that you talked with me."

Later, they went out to dinner.

Years later, another chancellor would publish a letter in the same archdiocesan paper. It decried the practice of group reconciliation. Within days, some seventy pastors gathered at Holy Name Cathedral's auditorium — the cardinal's own parish church — and formed a respectful but firm response. The matter died a quiet death soon after.

✠

Ted Stone was ordained in 1952, the same year as Bernardin. After a successful career working in catechetical ministry and pastoral studies, he resigned from the priesthood. He married and fathered two children.

In 1981 his wife died, leaving him with a nine-year-old son and a seven-year-old daughter. Two years later, his state job was eliminated. Six months later, he visited Bernardin and asked about the possibility of doing some pastoral work in a parish.

Bernardin told him that he would consider only a return to full ministry. Stone was overjoyed. Bernardin thought that the Vatican would look favorably on the petition.

He placed Ted in a parish where he took over the RCIA (Rite of Christian Initiation of Adults) program, social concerns, and ministry to the elderly.

The Vatican proved painfully slow. They were reluctant to reinstate anyone with minor children. The process took over six years. Stone was often close to telling the authorities to forget it. But Bernardin urged patience.

His case was stuck in the Office for the Doctrine of the Faith. The cardinal filed four petitions and numerous letters. Finally, he took a good portion of a private audience to speak to John Paul II. It loosened the log jam. Bernardin was told to write another letter. He returned to his room, wrote the letter by hand, and delivered it in person. The rescript came in a few weeks.

Fr. Ted Stone is now associate pastor of Mary Seat of Wisdom Parish in Park Ridge, Illinois. He lives nearby with his two children.

✠

The cardinal's only real exercise was walking. He played football in high school, although he couldn't have been very good. A classmate claimed that he was a wide receiver. The team must have been a disaster. But he loved to walk around his near north side neighborhood and on the grounds of the seminary at Mundelein.

One day, while walking Astor Street, he met a woman who obviously didn't know him. "My, you're so handsome," she said. "You're just beautiful."

The cardinal was embarrassed and flattered. With his balding head and protruding ears, he was no cover model. He thanked her graciously and walked on.

Some time after, he was returning to his home when he spotted her again. She was addressing a carriage horse that plied the upscale, historic neighborhood. "My, you're so handsome," the same woman was saying to the horse. "You're just beautiful."

✠

Misericordia North is a facility for some five hundred mentally — and often physically — disabled. The cardinal liked to go there. It was an island of honesty and love in a deceptive world. ("Congratulations," one cynical priest said to a newly consecrated bishop. "You'll never get a bad meal and no one will ever tell you the truth.")

Misericordia had just completed nine new homes, each housing eight higher-functioning residents. The cardinal came to bless the new homes. The residents were lined up in each house. Spontaneous and affectionate by nature, they had been cautioned not to slow the cardinal down in his trek through the newly created village.

But one resident could not control himself. "Hello, Joe," he said. 'We're glad you're here!"

During a later visit following his surgery, one resident piped:

"I'm glad you're better. You were taking up too much of our television time."

✠

Before his visit to Denver in 1993 to meet John Paul II, who would address thousands of teenagers, the cardinal was interviewed by Andrew Herrmann of the *Chicago Sun-Times*. "Today, sometimes people consider youth to be totally different from the way we used to be when we were young," he told Herrmann. "We're told that they're self-centered, concerned only about themselves. "But, in fact, I have found young people to be very, very generous," he continued. "We just have to listen to them. . . . You know, we don't have all the answers. Young people have some answers, too."

Then he asked Herrmann: "Want to anger young people? Call them the *future* of the church. They are also the present and that is something we have to acknowledge."

✠

During his trip to Denver to meet the pope, Bernardin found himself at the head of the line on the tarmac at the Denver airport. As the senior active American cardinal, he would greet the pope first. He was joined by President Bill Clinton and his wife, Hillary.

The pope's Alitalia plane was delayed sixteen minutes. Bernardin found himself waiting awkwardly with the most powerful leader in the Western world. Protocol and his own innate prudence kept the cardinal from introducing any topic. The president must steer the conversation.

Clearly, Mr. Clinton wasn't anxious to get into any discussion of issues. If he had any in mind, he would save them for the pope. Most problems are simply too complex to be talked about at a windy airport.

So for sixteen minutes the first Italian-American to lead a major diocese made small talk with the man from Little Rock, who had attended a Catholic elementary school and Georgetown University.

"I found Hillary interesting," he said later. He could carry on an adult conversation with her while protocol tied the tongues of the two leaders.

✠

In the mid-1970s, while still in Cincinnati, Bernardin came to realize that he was giving a higher priority to good works than to prayer. Sometime later, he confided as much to three younger priests, two of whom he had ordained. He told them that he was having difficulty with prayer and he asked their help.

"Are you sincere in what you request?" they asked, according to his posthumously published book, *The Gift of Peace* (Loyola University Press, 1997). "Do you really want to turn this around?"

"In very direct — even blunt terms — they helped me realize that as a priest and a bishop I was urging a spirituality on others that I was not fully practicing myself," he wrote. It proved a turning point in his life. He found that prayer could not be done on the run. It had to be part of his "quality time."

He decided to give God the first hour of his day. "Not only did this put my life in a new and uplifting perspective," he wrote. "I found that I was able to share the struggles of my own spiritual journey with others."

— SIX —

"My God,
How Can This Be?"

ON THE DAY that the charge of sexual abuse of a minor was finally obtained, Cardinal Bernardin read the ominous language in the document that had been filed with the Cincinnati Court and exclaimed: "My God, how can this be?" After his death, his director of legal services, John O'Malley, would recall: "At the time I considered this to be the voice of understandable confusion and concern. I now realize this was instinctively and truly a prayer."

On November 12, 1993, a thirty-four-year-old man, a onetime seminary student in Cincinnati, filed a suit against Cardinal Bernardin and another priest, accusing them of having sexually abused him seventeen years earlier. In an egregious example of rigged news gathering, Cable News Network (CNN) had obtained an exclusive interview with Steven J. Cook, a resident of Philadelphia and a man dying of AIDS. The interview had been carefully timed for the eve of the semiannual meeting of the National Conference of Catholic Bishops in Washington, D.C.

The tactic worked. Within a few hours, it was on every newscast in the country. In Chicago it might as well have been a repeat of the Great Chicago Fire.

My first thoughts were of a book Jean and I had given to the cardinal. It was a passalong gift, a large book of wood-

101

cuts depicting the Book of Job. The century-old book had been produced without text. The large, spare images were powerful representations of Job's agony.

Bernardin had taken the book to his library at his Mundelein residence. Later, he would tell us that in the midst of the abuse charges he had gathered a few close priest friends and studied the images. He didn't say what the experience had done for him, only that he had viewed the suffering face of Job.

✠

The route to the Cincinnati courtroom could be traced to 1985 when Jason Berry, a freelance investigative journalist from New Orleans, began writing about a priest named Gilbert Gauthe, from Lafayette, Louisiana. Months before, in the Autumn of 1984, Berry began hearing reports of the priest who had been abusing boys for some time. As a Catholic, Berry loved the church. As an expectant father, he was horrified for the abused children.

Berry soon began hearing of cases in other dioceses, most of them involving multiple victims. He hooked up with the *National Catholic Reporter*. Soon the paper reported on some dozen cases across the country. The effort strained the paper's resources to the limit. Investigative journalism can be terribly expensive. Further, when the series appeared, NCR lost hundreds of angry subscribers.

But the massive denial did not slow the number of cases. Between 1984 and 1992, four hundred Catholic priests were charged. Berry now estimates that over $500 million has been paid in settlements to victims. At least one source projects that $1 billion will be paid by the year 2000. One diocese, Santa Fe, New Mexico, was threatened with bankruptcy after paying out settlements. Nationally, most dioceses protested that the settlements weren't very high, but refused to reveal dollar amounts.

No other issue in recent years has caused the church to lose more credibility. The church has become the object of ridicule in many quarters. The news held one fascinated and then angered. The hypocrisy seemed to run so deep that it gave one the bends.

The issue opened a can of worms. The all-male priesthood was portrayed as one of the major factors. There were abuse cases in other denominations, but the majority of them involved a male minister with a female child. In the case of Catholic priests the pattern was generally a priest with a male child. Although there is no concrete evidence that gay priests were any more sexually active than heterosexual priests, it dragged the issue of homosexuality among priests kicking and screaming into the open. There were calls for a major restructuring of the recruitment process and seminary system and the discontinuance of mandatory celibacy.

After much denial, the bishops responded by forming an ad hoc committee on sexual abuse, headed by Bishop John F. Kinney of St. Cloud, Minnesota. But the bishops' conference resisted all efforts to establish a national policy. Local power, it seemed, was more important. Besides, some bishops remained in complete denial. Yet, Jeffrey Anderson, an attorney in St. Paul, Minnesota, who specializes in cases of sex abuse by priests, reported that there are now cases in every one of the nation's 188 dioceses. Sadder still, Anderson reported that he has yet to handle a case with a survivor who had not first tried to settle the matter within the church.

Survivors are still treated as perpetrators. The courts are not their first but rather their last resort. In spite of overwhelming evidence, one major archbishop responded: "We're not going to bankrupt this diocese by paying off these so-called victims!" Soon the tragic picture emerged of unsmiling bishops reading a prepared statement, taking no questions, surrounded by their staffs and their inevitable lawyer.

✠

It was 1993 before John Paul II spoke out publicly. "I fully share your sorrow and your concern, especially your concern for the victims so seriously hurt by these misdeeds," he said. For the pope, the gospel word "woe" had a special application to those who would abuse children. But the Holy Father remained somewhat defensive, taking time to criticize the media for sensationalizing the situation.

John Paul II's statement was released about a week after it had been read at a closed-door session of the June 1993 meeting of the bishops in New Orleans. It was at this meeting that then Archbishop (now Cardinal) William Keeler of Baltimore, then president of the NCCB, announced the formation of the ad hoc committee.

In Chicago Jeanne Miller, mother of a sexual abuse victim, founded VOCAL (Victims of Clergy Abuse Linkup, now called Linkup.) She was energized by the high-handed treatment she had received from the archdiocese, which continued to treat victims as perpetrators. Later, Barbara Blaine, now a Chicago attorney, founded SNAP (Survivors' Network of those Abused by Priests). "Jeanne broke it open," Barbara says. "That's the only reason the church deals with it at all."

Both Miller and Blaine had an uneven relationship with Bernardin. Each had met with him on occasion, but the outcomes were sometimes painful. Bernardin had agreed to attend a Linkup conference, then refused, citing what Miller regarded as a technicality. The conference was held with an empty chair on the stage.

Blaine met with Bernardin, but she didn't hesitate to picket outside the chancery office or outside a church where a priest abuser was being reinstalled as pastor. It often takes such efforts to get the attention of a stubborn church.

Jason Berry described his experiences in his book *Lead Us Not into Temptation* (Doubleday, 1992). It was the first of dozens of books that catalogued the growing cancer. Another author, Richard Sipe, a Maryland psychotherapist and author of *A Secret World: Sexuality and the Search for Celibacy* (Brunner-Mazel, 1990), wrote: "It is clear that the institutional church is in a preadolescent state of psychosexual development.... Sex generally is rigidly denied externally while secretly explored. The rigidity extends to strict rules of inclusion and exclusion. Control and avoidance are of primary concern."

Perhaps even more shocking than the abuse cases themselves were the revelations that the respective bishops had been well aware of the problem and had looked the other way, tolerated, covered up, or simply lied about an entire spectrum of activity among priests. Sadly, the sexual system that surrounds the clerical culture still fosters — even rewards — psychosexual immaturity.

✠

In Chicago after some false starts, Cardinal Bernardin set up a structure to deal with the problem. A committee of experts was appointed to review not only all pending cases but also those known to have happened in the past. He was only the second bishop, after Archbishop Raymond Hunthausen of Seattle, to put a mechanism in place.

In the months that followed some twenty Chicago priests were removed from office. A permanent "team" was put in place to review all subsequent allegations. Bernardin even installed an 800 number, intended for victims, available twenty-four hours each day. And the first thing Bernardin did after the accusations against him were made public was to submit all relevant material to the Review Board.

The cardinal's actions brought a mixed response. It raised a plethora of other issues. Some priests complained that he had gone too far, that they were being treated as property, and that basic causes of such behavior — poor growth experiences, depression, addiction, etc. — were not being addressed. The Association of Chicago Priests, while supporting the initiative, submitted an alternate set of policies, one that focused more on the priests' rights as citizens. But it was rejected.

The Bernardin model was offered to any diocese that wished to adopt it. Although it drew few callers, the cardinal stuck to his decision. His plan remains not fully developed. He was stuck with the "once a priest always a priest" doctrine, so he could not "fire" them. Besides, as one weary priest observed, "You would only turn a pedophile priest into a pedophile insurance man."

The process remains partly shrouded in secrecy, but it would seem that both offenders and victims are offered therapy, settlements are made, and the offending priests are being counseled out of the priesthood.

✠

My first news of the accusation against Bernardin came from an angry father of an alleged victim. He had been fighting the archdiocese for years, spending personal funds against the deep pockets of the archdiocese. The tactics used by the church's counsel did it little credit, and the father's anger had grown accordingly.

Even before he hung up, the news was reaching the evening reports. Not long after I heard the basic details of the charge, I received a called from National Public Radio (NPR). Among the questions they asked was a simple one: "Will this hurt the cardinal?"

I may have answered too quickly, but I still believe what I said. "Of course, it will," I answered. "Such a charge would hurt anyone, regardless of guilt or innocence." I went on to say that the Vatican is never pleased when a prelate is accused of any indiscretion. In their view the bishop is supposed to "handle" the matter, i.e., do anything it takes to avoid family shame. Innocent or not, Bernardin should have kept the matter under wraps.

When the cardinal's aides reported the matter to him, he was genuinely upset. Jean and I went out for dinner, but upon our return there was a pained message from him on our answering machine. "How could you say that, Tim?" he asked. "I'll call you later."

As we watched the 10:00 p.m. news, we saw the cardinal being driven from his mansion, allegedly to get away from the press. Our phone rang. It was Bernardin, asking again how I could have said such a thing. I answered that I said it because I believed it. He didn't share my cynicism, but he seemed less angry. I still trace some of his waning influence among his fellow cardinals to this accusation.

He called Tom Fox, editor of *National Catholic Reporter* and a man who had become a good friend to him. Fox later reported that he heard Bernardin's voice "in total isolation." "Tom," he said to Fox, "I don't even know the man [Cook]. I don't remember him. I've never abused anyone."

The hurried press conference was mobbed. Bernardin had already decided that he would play this drama out alone. "I'm going to do it my way," he said, rejecting the advice of some of his staff who believed that a statement from his lawyer would spare him some pain. "If they don't agree, they can leave." Instead, he entered the Chicago press conference alone, as he did all subsequent ones until he was cleared. "I'm going to answer all their questions. I'm innocent. I have nothing to hide."

In Washington the bishops' conference took a distant second place to the press conference held at the hotel. Again, Bernardin entered alone and answered a barrage of questions, some so utterly tasteless that they made reporters wince. ("Have you always been celibate?" was typical of the more invasive questions.)

I asked no questions but later did listen to many bishops

speaking on other topics in various rooms. None began their presentations without first making some statement of support for
the embattled cardinal. He was getting some support.

The wheels of justice ground slowly. Bernardin was a man
who would defend himself. An estimated ten lawyers in Cincinnati and Chicago worked on the case. They quickly reduced his
accuser's evidence to tatters.

✠

The case introduced the phenomenon of the delayed — or sup-
pressed or false — memory syndrome. It has to do with an
ugly memory that stays hidden for years until some event trig-
gers it and the person remembers. Steven Cook stated that his
memory had been awakened by an experience with a hypnotist,
whom it turned out, upon investigation, was utterly unqualified.
Dr. Harold Bush, a psychologist friend, informed me that he had
never encountered a case of this memory syndrome in anyone
over seventeen — and Cook was twice that age.

In the months that followed Bernardin told others that the
experience was the most difficult in his life. But he continued
to live an open life. At the Pastoral Center, an alley behind the
five-story building served as a parking lot for a few top officials,
including the cardinal. He could park, enter through a back door,
and travel unnoticed to his office. Instead, until he was cleared,
he insisted on parking directly outside the main entrance. He did
not want to be accused of ducking the press.

On March 1, 1994, Steven Cook called a press conference and
recanted his charge. He said that his memory was "unreliable."
He could not go forward. Clearly, there was more to the case.
A close priest friend of Bernardin's said: "You bet there was!"
But whatever else was under investigation, it did not involve
Bernardin. It never had. He was cleared.

Months later, Bernardin flew to Philadelphia, where Steven

Cook was near death. There was forgiveness and reconciliation. He said Mass for Cook and gave him the Eucharist. Cook died soon after.

Early in the drama, a close friend of Jean's went to her doctor for a routine visit. Although both were Jewish, they talked of the only topic on anyone's mind in November 1993: the accusation. Knowing the toll that stress can take, the doctor did not hesitate to make a prediction: "He'll get cancer," the doctor said. "He'll get cancer."

— SEVEN —

The Search for
a Common Ground

S OMETIME AFTER 1984, Cardinal Bernardin's influence began to wane. Earlier, in a cover story following the release of the bishops' pastoral *The Challenge of Peace,* of which he was the principal author, *Time* magazine had called him "the most influential bishop in America." Adjectives such as "liberal," and "consensus builder" were used to describe his style.

The pastoral letter, although approved by the conference of bishops at a special meeting in Chicago in May 1983, was tied to Bernardin. It was not without its critics among his fellow bishops. They were largely men educated to a precise definition of just war dating to the days of spears and arrows. Bishop John O'Connor, a retired rear admiral and former chief of chaplains in the U.S. Navy, was on the ad hoc Committee of War and Peace and had differed with Bernardin on virtually every paragraph. "O'Connor is a decent fellow," Bernardin would observe privately. "We [the committee] gave him a few things in the document."

In 1983 O'Connor was bishop of Scranton, Pennsylvania, a diocese of 362,000 Catholics. After less than a year in Scranton, John Paul II leapfrogged him to New York, the cash register of the American Catholic Church, with a Catholic population of

2.3 million. Meanwhile, Bishop Bernard F. Law of Springfield–Cape Girardeau, Missouri, the son of a United States Air Force colonel, was plucked from the little diocese (52,000 Catholics) to head one of the country's oldest sees. Boston had been established as a diocese in 1808 and had already been awarded three red hats. It was home to nearly 2 million Catholics and, like New York, had excellent universities and a priest corps that was so rich it often supplied other dioceses. Yet neither archdiocese could claim to be a seedbed of ideas.

Law and O'Connor received the red hat at a consistory held on May 25, 1985. Both men gained a reputation as spokesmen for John Paul II's emphasis on doctrinal and organizational constancy, rather than pastoral flexibility. Both men appeared to have the pope's ear on episcopal appointments.

Meanwhile, in the Midwest, it appeared that Bernardin was unable to influence appointments even within the province of Illinois over which he presided. In 1987 John J. Myers, an arch-conservative, was appointed bishop of Peoria, Illinois, and in 1994, Thomas Doran, a Vatican bureaucrat, was picked over Bernardin's choice, Robert E. Morneau, auxiliary bishop of Green Bay, Wisconsin, to head the Rockford diocese. Both dioceses virtually border on Chicago.

Yet, while the Vatican searched for what one critic described as "office managers," when bishops began butting miters, it was to Bernardin they turned to settle impasses. Typically, when O'Connor and Law disavowed a statement on AIDS issued by the NCCB's administrative board, Bernardin steered the hierarchy clear of an embarrassing showdown. The two cardinals were calling for an unqualified ban on any education on AIDS, especially information about condoms. Bernardin yielded to the conservative cardinals on the use of condoms, but managed to address a wide variety of AIDS-related issues.

It was in this same spirit — and against even more opposition — that the now dying cardinal introduced what became known as his Common Ground Project: on August 12 he released a new statement, *Called to Be Catholic: Church in a Time of Peril.*

As always, it was at another sunshine conference with all the media invited. The press wasn't certain just what the conference was all about. When it ended, most were still not certain. On the previous day, I had lunch with Fr. Peter Bowman, vicar for administration and moderator of the cardinal's curia. Although the third-ranking administrator of the archdiocese and a man with a nose for news, Bowman himself wasn't certain what Bernardin would announce. When he went out on a limb, the cardinal often went alone. He didn't want his staff to be hurt if the limb broke or was sawed off by reactionaries.

"I have been troubled that an increasing polarization within the church and, at times, a mean-spiritedness have hindered the kind of dialogue that helps us address our mission and concerns," he began. "As a result, the unity of the church is threatened, the great gift of the Second Vatican Council is in danger of being seriously undermined, the faithful members of the church are weary, and our witness to government, society, and culture is compromised."

He then went on to announce the inauguration of what he called the Catholic Common Ground Project. It was an endeavor inspired by *Called to Be Catholic: Church in a Time of Peril,* which had been prepared by the National Pastoral Life Center in New York in consultation with Bernardin and other leaders who had joined him in the initiative. The center is a research and consultation group headed by Msgr. Philip J. Murnion.

Bernardin considered the Common Ground Project just one attempt to respond to the statement. "Using the teaching of the Second Vatican Council as its basis for dialogue," Bernardin told the reporters, "this project will sponsor conferences that bring together persons of divergent perspectives in search of a 'Catholic

Common Ground.'" He had gathered a committee of twenty-four and stated that he hoped to hold the first conference in the spring of 1997.

The first meeting was to focus on the relationship between the church and culture in the U.S. It would be developed within the context one of the most significant of the sixteen documents of Vatican II, *The Pastoral Constitution of the Church in the Modern World* (*Gaudium et Spes*).

The *Called to Be Catholic* statement was remarkably strong. Its authors had to know that it would wrinkle some watered silk, especially in those dioceses that viewed themselves as custodians of truth. "American Catholics must reconstitute the conditions for addressing our differences constructively," the statement read. There must be "a common ground centered on faith in Jesus, marked by accountability to the living Catholic tradition and ruled by a new spirit of civility, dialogue, generosity, and broad and serious consultation."

The statement went on to cite fourteen varied issues, such as a crisis in religious illiteracy, the drift of young people away from the sacraments, the changing roles of women, and the ways in which the church's teaching can contribute to the development of public policy. It even asked for dialogue on the very survival of Catholic institutions.

"Unless we examine our situation with fresh eyes, open minds, and changed hearts," the statement read, "within a few decades a vital Catholic legacy may be squandered, to the loss of both the church and the nation."

In strong language the document points out that "in almost every case, the necessary conversation runs up against polarized positions that have so magnified fears and so strained sensitivities that even the simplest lines of inquiry are often fiercely resisted." The statement then called for a search for and rediscovery of some common ground — a place that would encompass all whether they be centrists, moderates, liberals, radicals, conservatives, or neo-conservatives. The melting pot of Catholics would then reaffirm basic truths and pursue their disagreements "in a renewed spirit of dialogue."

"Our faith and our common life as members of the community of faith, which is the church, are indeed great and precious gifts," Bernardin concluded. "Let us together leave behind whatever brings discord.... Let us walk in communion with, and in loyalty to, our Holy Father in order to restore and strengthen the unity that has been fractured or diminished."

✠

It was both a statement and a plea. Bernardin abhorred discord. He was weary of pickets on the right or left circling outside the Pastoral Center. He was sometimes shocked at the virulent hatred that religion seemed to unleash. He simply wanted people to live the Gospel in relative peace and harmony.

His twenty-four-member committee was composed of himself, eight bishops, and fifteen other clergy, religious, and lay people. It was heavily elitist. There was a former governor, university professors, lawyers, an editor of *Commonweal*, a union president, and the head of a major congregation of religious women. Only five were women and three of them were religious.There was a broad geographical distribution but few minorities.

Bernardin was bemused by the criticism of the committee's makeup. He felt that, although most were tied to the church through vocation and paycheck, these people could embrace all levels of Catholic thinking. He might have been naive in this; cardinals do tend to inhabit elite worlds. But he quickly promised to expand the committee. He repeatedly reminded his questioners that this was a committee on a search and that the agenda remained open.

He had worked on the project for over three years. He

hadn't created a legislative group, just one that would engage in constructive dialogue. He knew well that Paul VI, perhaps his favorite pope, had used the word "dialogue" no less than sixty-seven times in his 1964 encyclical, *Ecclesiam Suam* (On the Church). He realized that institutional religion was a game of inches.

Not many questions followed his announcement. Few religion reporters are that sophisticated. Most honestly didn't know quite what he was talking about. TV reporters, in particular, struggled to reduce his somewhat vague and complicated statements to a few sound bytes.

One well-informed journalist whispered to me: "He's too vague. What are the expected outcomes? Who else gets to come?" In a world where virtually every tie game goes into overtime, Bernardin's lofty concept that people of differing viewpoints could sit down together, learn from each other, and find areas of agreement, was lost. In the view of his conservative critics, for example, he might as well have been nailing his modest proposal to the doors of Wittenberg Cathedral.

Bernardin was reduced to answering questions about whether or not other bishops knew about this initiative. He replied that he had informed the Vatican and the apostolic delegate and had not yet received a reply. He had informed the other major prelates but had received responses only from a few moderates such as Anthony M. Pilla, bishop of Cleveland and president of the National Conference of Catholic Bishops. The bishops on the committee took a risk. Their presence on the roster could short circuit their careers or at least diminish their influence. Yet, Cardinal Roger Mahony of Los Angeles, Archbishops Oscar Lipscomb of Mobile, Daniel Pilarczyk of Cincinnati, and Rembert Weakland of Milwaukee risked being tarred with the same brush as Bernardin. (His link with Mahony, the youngest cardinal in the U.S., may have cemented a relationship that caused him to select the Californian to preside at his funeral.)

Other reporters asked if groups such as Call to Action, a liberal group, and Catholics United for the Faith, a conservative group, would be represented. Bernardin responded that "representative individuals" would be invited, not representative groups. He stressed that no decision had been made as to precisely who would be invited to the conferences, only that the first one would be in Chicago and that "nothing would be done secretly or behind closed doors."

He seemed a little bewildered. The statement had been carefully drawn and precisely worded. He may have forgotten the fact that, while he had spent days on the project, the media was hearing it for the first time. He pleaded that the committee was still feeling its way and that he simply didn't know all the answers about structure and process.

While the media knew that he was dying, no one had any idea that his death would occur just three months later. Asked if his death sentence would hobble the project, Bernardin responded that the project "no longer depended upon him."

The press conference ended after only a few more awkward questions. Bernardin seemed relieved. But he had no idea of the criticism that was to follow.

✠

There were groups outside the Pastoral Center even before the press conference ended. Each was carving out its territory. Only Call to Action, a liberal, Chicago-based, nationwide group, appeared ready to join Bernardin on the Common Ground he had attempted to stake out. Linda Pieczynski, president of CTA, said that Bernardin "has proposed constructing a bridge of communication over troubled waters in our church, and we applaud him for the personal witness of hope, courage, and respect for others' opinions that he brings to the task."

Although Bernardin had stressed that the conference discussions would be within the framework of authentic church teaching, his very announcement was viewed as a deviation from the chain-of-command, highly institutional understanding of church. "Authentic accountability rules out a fundamentalism that narrows the richness of the tradition to a text or a decree," his statement read, "and it rules out a narrow appeal to individual or contemporary experience that ignores the cloud of witnesses over the centuries or the living magisterium of the church." Although he was calling all to witness the richness of authentic teaching, his critics viewed this appeal to the teaching authority as a threat to it.

Perhaps what stung the cardinal the most was the swift and cold reaction of his fellow cardinals. Although prelates rarely disagree in public, when they do, protocol demands that they telephone their fellow cardinal with whom they disagree and attempt to find some wiggle room. Instead, Cardinals Bernard Law (Boston), James Hickey (Washington), Adam Maida (Detroit), and Anthony Bevilacqua (Philadelphia) released strong objections to the document. New York's John O'Connor refrained, although his archdiocesan paper, *Catholic New York,* ran an unsigned editorial critical of Project Common Ground. Later, through a spokesman, O'Connor vigorously denied that he had even read the editorial before its appearance. However, observers quickly reasoned that the editor clearly reflected the mind of the archbishop. It left only William Keeler (Baltimore) as the only cardinal who did not comment.

Bernardin's brother cardinals were respectful. They did not question motives. They weren't sharp-tongued or acrimonious. But it was clear that they all ran for high ground, speaking forth truths that Bernardin never questioned at all. Law wrote: "The crisis the church is facing can only be adequately addressed by a clarion call to conversion." Maida said he believed that such issues could not be solved by dialogue, "but rather through conversion which is the result of prayer and fasting." Bevilacqua

stated: "Rather what is needed is that common vision illumi-
nated through prayer to see Jesus as he himself asked to be seen:
the way, the truth, and the life." So it went. The cardinals' cautionary statements only served to distort the Common Ground
paper. Bernardin had never questioned the issues they raised.

It was dialogue that the cardinals feared most. "Dissent from
revealed truth of the authoritarian teaching of the church cannot be 'dialogued' away," Law wrote. "Truth and dissent are not
equal partners in ecclesial dialogue." Washington's Hickey said
that there cannot be dissent from church teaching, or else we
forfeit our common ground. Maida observed that Bernardin's
paper suggested "that Catholic teachings are open to dialogue
and debate." It was clear that the Eastern bloc cardinals were
frightened.

✠

Bernardin, now growing weaker, tried to respond. On August 29,
he issued a ten-page written statement that pleaded that his call
for dialogue in the church was not an invitation to dissent or
compromise with the truth. He pointed out that he expected
criticisms "from some groups on the right or left" who judge
everything in terms of their own agenda. But he appeared clearly
surprised and hurt by the polite savaging by his fellow cardinals.
"Even the carefully framed appeal for dialogue coming from a
broad range of distinguished advisors," he wrote, "was met by
immediate suspicion." The major criticisms Bernardin received
charged him with failing to adequately acknowledge Scripture,
tradition, and the centrality of Jesus. Further, his critics held that
the paper placed dissent and truth at the same level.

On the same weekend in which he announced that his cancer was terminal, several of the cardinals, who had criticized his
proposal in what many observers thought was an organized effort, came to Chicago for a religious book conference. "I greeted

them," Bernardin told me later. "Cardinal Law was most concerned about me. I just let his criticism go." Earlier, Law had invited him to come to Boston for what both hoped was a period of recuperation. Law, and his fellow cardinals, are conservative but not unkind. Bernardin ended his response by simply saying: "I am convinced that a careful reading of the text ought to reassure those who expressed these concerns."

The first conference was scheduled for the spring, but Bernardin asked that one be held as soon as possible in order to insure an orderly transfer of leadership. As promised, it was an open meeting but the pre-conference publicity was weak. Only a little more than 250 people came to the Sheraton Chicago Hotel and Towers for the meeting. The room appeared half-empty.

"A dying person does not have time for the peripheral or the accidental," the weakened cardinal told the group. "He or she is drawn to the essential, the important — yes, the eternal."

Twenty-three members of the twenty-four-member committee attended the meeting, a remarkable figure since they are high-powered busy people from all parts of the nation. Bernardin used the occasion to name Archbishop Oscar Lipscomb of Mobile, Alabama, as his successor as chairman. He pledged that the work would continue.

The conference was a booster shot for Bernardin. Committee member Michael Novak, a conservative thinker, acknowledged that he had serious reservations about the project but that he was convinced that he could do the church a service by helping to clarify the debate on major issues such as human sexuality, the priesthood, and the collision of modern culture and church teachings.

What pleased Bernardin the most was the announcement by Msgr. Murnion that the National Pastoral Life Center had received "an enormous number of letters and phone calls from people who were moved by the announcement."

Still, his critics haunted him. One man observed: "Hey, if

Bernardin hadn't had those sexual abuse charges and his cancer, he would just be another bishop." Another, saying that he represented the Veritatis Forum, a little known conservative group, said that he saw the Common Ground Project as a way to water down the true teachings of the church. "These people should be excommunicated from the church," he added. "They're not really Catholic." Soon after the responses began pouring in, Bernardin observed wryly: "Who says there's no dissent in the church?"

Later, reviewing his efforts during an interview with the *New York Times Magazine,* he said: "I've tried to create a climate in which people get along with each other. There are people at the extremes who are just as angry with me and the church now as they were when I came [to Chicago], but I think I've gotten people to accept each other a little bit better. I've given people permission to be themselves. They know that they're not going to get their heads chopped off if they're candid or if they don't measure up."

— EIGHT —

The Final Days

FROM AUGUST 30, the day he announced that he would die within a year or less, until 1:33 a.m. on the morning of November 14, Cardinal Bernardin's life took another turn. Now the weary cliché concerning "the things of this world" became a searing reality. He would die within a year — most likely much sooner. He had spent his priesthood teaching people how to live. Now he would teach them how to die.

Bernardin enjoyed life. He loved a good meal, including a good bottle of wine to follow his Scotch or Campari. His favorite restaurant was likely Daniel J's, a small but high-quality restaurant on the city's north side. It is owned by Mary and Jack Jones, who became close friends of the cardinal. Jack is a professional chef; Mary is a former teacher in a Catholic high school. The meals were creative; the prices within Bernardin's prudent range. Typically, he embraced Mary and Jack. They became friends and, when they expressed the wish to adopt a child, Bernardin put his considerable weight behind the application.

The cardinal had an eye for what was tasteful — it was one reason why he liked Paul VI, who had filled whole galleries in the Vatican Museum with powerful modern art. Although pretty much confined to clerical garb, his occasional casual dress reflected a person of taste.

He loved being with people, especially close friends. He enjoyed travel, especially to Italy and England. (Cardinal George Basil Hume, O.S.B., archbishop of Westminster, was a close friend, and a wealthy Chicago family supplied him with a London flat.) He loved his North State Parkway mansion and his other mansion on the grounds of the seminary at Mundelein, both built by predecessors. He would never have built such enormous triumphalist monuments himself, but he put them to good use for social and fundraising purposes. He enjoyed playing host at the Chicago mansion to a procession of visiting dignitaries and friends, including the First Lady, Hillary Clinton, and a virtual conclave of visiting cardinals. ("I haven't figured him out yet," he said candidly of one traveling cardinal, "but he seems like a good bishop.") He talked occasionally of acquiring a summer home, but never got around to it. Somehow, the Depression-era kid and the priest within him kept him from too much luxury. He liked nice things but didn't covet them.

Clearly, this was not a man who wanted to die. In fact, during the final three years of his life, he appeared to be more confident, relaxed, and carefree. He was consciously beginning to sort things out. "You know," he said to a group of priests gathered for a presbyteral senate meeting, "I'm beginning to think that at least 20 percent of what I do is a waste of time." ("Not 20 percent," one wag answered. "At least 80 percent.")

He appeared to have grown impatient with bureaucratic sluggishness; he could even reflect some measured anger at Vatican attitudes that often treated any appeal to their authority as a challenge to it. I once said to him that I sometimes got the feeling that he wished that his priests would simply make pastoral decisions without clearing them. He nodded in agreement. It was obvious that he found it painful to remind a pastor that he had overstepped some nearly invisible line.

On occasion when a pastor did overstep reasonable lines to meet pastoral needs, Bernardin would urge: "Please, don't do this. I can't support you. Don't make me discipline you."

The professional bishop within him was gone. "Listen," he told his two top aides, Bishop Raymond Goedert, vicar general, and Fr. Peter Bowman, vicar for administration, "we're in our late sixties. Our careers have ended. We're not going anywhere. Let's run this archdiocese the way we would want to see it run."

Now, in the words of one priest observer, "he no longer felt the need to face Rome. Now he could face Lake Michigan."

At the close of his press conference, I touched his arm and said to him: "We're heartbroken." I'm not certain that he heard me. He simply turned and said: "I'm coming."

He was referring to our annual dinner date, scheduled for Sunday, September 1, two days away and the last time we would have a lengthy conversation with him. We had already written him and told him to feel no obligation about coming — although we selfishly hoped that he would, regardless of his condition.

He arrived in his gray Buick precisely on time. He had called from his car phone moments before, announcing that he would arrive in "six or seven minutes." Bernardin was that way — as obsessive compulsive about time as he was about everything else.

He was dressed casually in perfectly matching shirt and slacks and spit-polish loafers. In earlier years he was cautious about going public in mufti. In his final years he seemed to enjoy it, especially when he realized that people were relieved to see him so relaxed.

I waited for him in the lobby of our building, located two miles north of his mansion. There is always traffic in and out and, within seconds of his arrival, his familiar face had drawn a small crowd. They were a mixed group, largely Jewish, but they could have been parishioners. Knowing of our friendship with him, they often asked: "How's our cardinal doing?"

As he entered our condominium home, he announced: "I'll answer any questions except those about my successor." We promised discretion but observed it only weakly.

"Where are they going to put you?" I asked. "I'll go to Mount

Carmel," he said, without a trace of resentment at my tastelessly worded question. "In 1988 they brought me out there to pick my spot. I'll be just to the left of Cardinal Cody."

Mount Carmel is an enormous cemetery. Opened in 1901, it has at least a thousand burials each year. Shortly after it was opened, its first two hundred acres were filled. The influenza epidemic of 1918 saw seventy-five burials each day. In the early years there was little discipline in the arrangement of burial plots. Church authorities were too busy simply preparing enough space for the internment of the population avalanche. As a result, care of graves was often left to families and the type of memorial was also left to the plot holder. The result was a melange of virtually unmarked graves mixed with elaborate mausoleums, over four hundred of them, many owned by Italian families. In time, and unfairly, the cemetery became known as the "Arlington National Cemetery of the Mafia." There is a particle of truth in this image. Al Capone is buried there. But, after Bernardin's death, observers expressed the hope that the Italian-American bishop would highlight the vast majority of Italians who were resting there — people much closer to the Bernardin model than to the scarred model of a handful of miscreants.

The Bishops' Mausoleum is an elaborate pile, done in a Romanesque style with intricate — and beautiful — mosaics on the ceiling. They may be a bit too much for Bernardin's taste. But the fact that the mausoleum is closed much of the time has served to preserve the brilliant colors. It was begun in 1905 under Archbishop James E. Quigley (1903–15) and not finished until 1912. It was built to hold seventeen bishops, likely enough to last another century. Bernardin is the seventh to be buried there. Cardinals Mundelein and Meyer are buried at the Seminary of St. Mary of the Lake. Mundelein had built the place. Indeed, the entire village, once a bucolic rural town called Area, was named after him, partly in gratitude for a fire engine he gave the village. Albert Meyer had taught in the Milwaukee seminary, enough of a qualification to permit him to be buried on the seminary grounds.

Above the massive bronze doors, carved into the marble, is the single Latin word *Resurrecturis* ("to those who will rise again"). For years, memorial Masses were celebrated there, but now the priest shortage, fewer worshipers, and a certain sense that such private Masses were no longer the highest and best use of a priest's gifts have caused the place to be closed much of the time. Following Bernardin's funeral, it was opened for a week. Later, the church agreed to open it on Sundays. In the first few days following his burial, fifteen thousand visitors came.

✠

The cardinal wasn't complaining about the mausoleum, but I think the stonemason's son might have preferred a plain black basalt monument with simply the name "Bernardin" on it. He might also have preferred burial in Holy Name Cathedral, but the relatively small building has no room for resting bishops.

His final months were surprisingly productive in spite of the fact that one of the symptoms of pancreatic cancer is a progressive weariness that leaves one utterly spent. When he arrived at our home, he was driving his own car but walking cautiously. He asked for a pillow to support his back, but otherwise appeared fit. As always, he accepted a drink and sipped wine during a meal of salmon, pasta, and roasted vegetables.

Over dinner, he confided with almost childlike glee that he had just been informed by President Clinton that he was to receive the Presidential Medal of Freedom. It is the nation's highest civilian award, established in 1963 by John F. Kennedy. Kennedy selected the first recipients but was assassinated before he could make the presentations. Early winners included Marian Anderson (contralto), Pablo Casals (cellist), George Meany (labor leader), Thurgood Marshall (public servant), and Colin

Powell (soldier). Religious leaders have been extremely rare and Bernardin has been the sole Catholic recipient. As always, he expected to be criticized by conservatives and single-issue Catholics for accepting the award. He had long grown used to it.

"Don't tell anyone," he said. It was a tidbit served to a number of friends with the same warning. The cardinal was known as someone from whom secrets could not be pried. But, especially with good news, he could leak like a sieve. A story is told at the chancery that a concerted effort was made by some worried administrators to plug leaks by first finding their source and putting the offender on notice. When they discovered that Brother Joseph was the source of the leak, they gave up.

During the ceremony President Clinton called Bernardin "one of our nation's most beloved men and one of Catholicism's great leaders." The cardinal accepted the award but used the occasion to speak in Washington about his consistent ethic of life theme. He might have spoken up gently but firmly at the ceremony itself, but protocol requires that recipients remain silent.

Following the ceremony, during a speech at Georgetown University, he stated that "each life is of infinite value," and that he is in "fundamental disagreement with President Clinton." Again, Bernardin did not draw the line after abortion. He extended his seamless garment over all of life, including the recent issues of assisted suicide and late-term abortions. Privately he had told me that he liked President Clinton, but that they disagreed sharply on life issues. He was very concerned, however, that the bishops' positions on these issues would place them in the Republican camp.

✠

Within the next few weeks, he would complete the manuscript of a small book — *The Gift of Peace* — that would appear following his death. It digested the experiences of his final three years, focusing on the sexual abuse charges and his illness.

He turned over the management of archdiocesan affairs to his vicar, Bishop Raymond Goedert, but before doing so he completed a detailed report to the Vatican on the conduct of his see. He also updated his will and made arrangements for the care of his mother following his death. "I wanted her to die before me," he said often. It was the nature of things and also tied to his personality of keeping things tidy. His friend, Msgr. Ken Velo, would take over the responsibility for the care of his mother.

Bernardin also wrote three significant letters. One was to his fellow bishops, who were holding their annual meeting at the Omni Shoreham Hotel in Washington, D.C. The conference had been gradually turning to the right for years, and a number of bishops wanted desperately to rid the conference of lay or media involvement. While the number of strongly conservative bishops was relatively few — an estimated 50 to 80 of some 180 voting bishops and several hundred other auxiliary and retired bishops, they were persistent and vocal, speaking against one resolution after another and hoping to return the conference to an exclusively episcopal group.

Bernardin's presence would have energized the more moderate bishops. Instead, Bishop Anthony Pilla of Cleveland, president of the conference, read the handwritten note to the group in which Bernardin asked them for their prayers "that God will give me the strength and grace I need each day."

Some bishops at the conference wondered aloud who could take Bernardin's place. In what appeared to be a collegial decision, all of the bishops refused to speculate on his successor. Typical of the statements was one by Bishop Nicolas C. Dattilo of Harrisburg, Pennsylvania. "He's been so much a part of the conference," he said. "It's a loss for the church because he's a relatively young man filled with energy and a love for the Lord."

Retired Archbishop John Quinn of San Francisco said: "There

will be no one to take his place. There is no one with his combi-
nation of experience." Quinn and Bernardin were good friends.
Quinn had been president of the NCCB. He and Bernardin
worked together on the dispute in Seattle involving Archbishop
Raymond Hunthausen. Bernardin was compared by some bishops with his mentor, Cardinal John Dearden of Detroit, who had
died at age eighty in 1988, coincidentally of pancreatic cancer.
The bishops gave the cardinal a two-minute standing ovation.
One said, "I hope he hears us."

Ever the teaching bishop, he wrote a formal letter to the U.S.
Supreme Court in which he urged the justices — three of them
Catholic — to reject arguments that the dying have a right to
a physician-assisted suicide. "As one who is dying," he wrote, "I
have especially come to appreciate the gift of life. Creating a new
right to assisted suicide would endanger society and send a false
signal that a less than 'perfect' life is not worth living." The letter
was submitted on November 12 as part of a friend-of-the-court
brief by the Catholic Health Association of the United States.
The court was scheduled to hear arguments in 1997 on two cases
that ask whether the Constitution grants terminally ill patients a
right to kill themselves with the physician's help. "Even a person who decides to forgo treatment does not necessarily choose
death," Bernardin added. "Rather, he chooses life without the
burden of disproportionate medical intervention."

The appeal was classic Bernardin — respectful, direct, clear
but not confrontational. He did not engage in *ad hominem* at-
tacks. He assumed that the nine justices on the nation's highest
court were people of good faith and good heart, even if an
adverse decision was handed down.

✠

His final effort was his Christmas cards. Always the detail person, he had prepared his list but wanted to add personal notes

to at least some of the cards. A close personal friend, Fr. Scott Donahue, associate director for Mercy Boys and Girls Home, urged him to mail the cards early. Bernardin appeared relieved. Once he learned that they had been mailed, he was reported to have said: "Good, I can go now."

His penchant for detail was an internal joke. At his funeral, his homilist, Msgr. Ken Velo, told a packed cathedral that he sent "thank you" cards to people who sent him "thank you" cards.

In a relatively minor issue, a Chicago night club had been using a logo that was remarkably like the famous Sacred Heart image, the one with the crown of thorns surrounding it and the flaming heart above. Such graphic art was not the Bernardin style but he understood that the image was held sacred by many. He wrote a letter to the club's owner and urged its removal. Following negotiations with church officials, it was altered to something less offensive.

His Christmas card contained a hand-written and reproduced note that said in part: "This is a very special Christmas for me because it is likely my last on this earth. There is, of course, a tinge of sadness in this reality. But there is also joy and anticipation at the prospect of being more intimately united with the Lord in the world to come....When I begin my final journey home, know that I will carry you in my heart."

The note was perfect Bernardin. Generally, people of his vintage can hardly write a sentence without at least one fractured word or missing comma. His was perfect. It would be hard to believe that it was written by a man who could hardly stand. The card, written earlier, was in stark contrast to his note to his fellow bishops, written on November 10, a few days before his death. His handwriting was shaky. The final paragraph in particular was difficult to read. His final sentence to the bishops — "My only request to them is that they pray that God will give me the strength and grace I need each day" — was very hard to decipher. Clearly, his hand was shaking.

Reaction to the Christmas card demonstrated the virtual cult that was growing around the cardinal. Two newspapers called me and asked if I had one that they could reproduce. A TV station asked me to comment on camera and to "bring the Christmas card."

In the weeks that followed the media did turn him into a cult figure. There were interviews with people who had only a thin relationship with him. He received thousands of letters, many from elementary school children, written during class hours. During the early stages of his illness, he received so many letters — one source said "over ten thousand," — that he had to bring his former secretary, Octavie Mosimann, out of retirement to handle the crush.

During a visit to the Pastoral Center, the security guard pointed out a pile of notes and small items that the cardinal had been asked to sign. They had to be returned without his signature. He had not been to the Pastoral Center in several weeks.

Bernardin himself received an autographed football from the Chicago Bears and their devoutly Catholic coach, Dave Wannstedt. Each happening was treated as an epiphany and reported with great drama. The media couldn't get enough of this shy man who was dying in such a public way. His life had taken him to a fate he shared with everyone. He was going to die. By teaching others how to die, he could bond with everyone. "Americans will talk about anything, except their salary and death," one cynic said. The dying prelate gave people permission to talk about death. People who could barely compose a sentence about the archbishop could talk about the man who was going to die. Those who were hoping for a miracle were overlooking the moral miracle happening all around them. Within days of the cardinal's funeral, a physician in nearby Merrillville, Indiana, called Gary bishop, Dale J. Melczak, and informed him that he would never perform another abortion; he admitted to having performed hundreds of them within the past two years. Elsewhere, dying people were at peace.

✠

During the year that followed his surgery, his "parish" of fellow cancer sufferers grew to over seven hundred people. He promised no miracles; he simply urged them to let death be. The cardinal had not come to this attitude lightly. He was frightened of death. He had told me and many others that he had often awakened at night, alone, frightened and in tears.

Just a few weeks before, a death row inmate had requested to see the dying cardinal. The man had been on death row for some twelve years. All appeals had been exhausted and he was facing death by lethal injection.

Although there remained the possibility that the convict was using him, Bernardin visited the man, a non-Catholic, and prayed with him. As expected, it brought criticism. "I told him we had one thing in common," Bernardin said, "we both were under sentence of death."

More honors poured in. An ecumenical group awarded him its first annual Common Ground Award. The award itself had been named after his Common Ground Project. Bernardin was now too ill to attend. Fr. Thomas Baima, director of ecumenical and religious affairs for the archdiocese, accepted on his behalf.

By now, the cardinal had gotten so weak that he was in constant pain. At one point, not long before he died, the spinal stenosis (compression) and osteoporosis in his back were so advanced that when he simply bent over to pick something up, he broke a rib. Yet he never once asked publicly, "Why me?"

As he lay dying, his close associate Bishop Raymond Goedert passed the long vigil and staved off grief by reviewing the proof sheets of *The Gift of Peace*. In there, he found Bernardin saying: "One of the things I have noticed about illness is that it draws you inside yourself. When we are ill, we tend to focus on our own pain and suffering. We may feel sorry for ourselves and become depressed. . . . My decision to discuss my cancer openly and honestly has sent a message that when we are ill, we need not close in on ourselves, or remove ourselves from others. Instead, it is during these times when we need people the most."

✠

In September 1995 I had written him about the possibility of doing a book, something along the lines of Henri Nouwen's small book that traced his own near death experience. Nouwen was a Dutch theologian who had taught at Harvard, Yale, and the University of Notre Dame. He had written some forty books and was a well-known speaker and retreat master. I suggested the possibility of his doing the book with Nouwen or with me. We shared the same publisher. Nouwen had abandoned much of his teaching and was living in Ontario, Canada, working at a home for the adult retarded. He had been the victim of a pedestrian-auto accident. His brush with death resulted in a moving book about death and dying. He died himself in September 1996 of a heart attack while visiting the Netherlands en route to Russia.

Bernardin responded to my letter on October 2, 1995. He wrote that he had "not settled in my own mind the kind of book I want written. . . . I need more time to see what the ultimate results will be. I need more time to recuperate," he added in the same letter. "Already I am doing more than I should. Once people see you looking good and moving around, the pressures are enormous." The correspondence may have prompted him to contact Fr. Nouwen, who counseled him, just as Bernardin himself would later counsel others.

By Monday, November 11, Bernardin knew for certain that he was entering his final hours. His oncologist, Dr. Ellen Gaynor, had answered him honestly, assuring him that he would be dead by Christmas. "Good," he said. "I'm ready." He reminded one of a person waiting at a train station, his bags all packed, waiting for the train to pull into the station.

One of his closest friends, Fr. Cletus Kiley, a former chancellor and rector of the college seminary, visited. Kiley, now pastor of St. Agnes of Bohemia Parish, had traveled often with the cardinal. He reported to Andrew Herrmann, a religion writer for the *Chicago Sun-Times*, that Bernardin looked weak but was in good spirits. "Well, I'm ready," Kiley reported the cardinal's words. "I hope it's not too long now because I'm ready."

On Sunday, Bishop Goedert told him that he would shortly be leaving for the bishops' conference in Washington. It was then that Bernardin struggled to his feet, went to his desk, and wrote the shaky note. Goedert did go to the conference but returned after only one day when informed by Msgr. Velo that the cardinal had taken a drastic turn for the worse. He returned to Chicago with another auxiliary bishop, Thad Jakubowski.

Death from pancreatic or liver cancer can be compared with the rapid turn of a dimmer switch. Once stricken by cancer, the liver can no longer clear toxic chemicals from the body. According to *Newsweek*'s cover essay on Bernardin, titled "Teaching Us How to Die," a poisonous metabolite of ammonia builds up in the blood. When the toxic compound reaches the brain, it kills neurons in the brain stem, which controls heartbeat and respiration. The patient lapses into a coma. Consciousness fades away. There is neither pain nor other sensation. Death follows within hours.

Given the arsenal of medications available, there is no excuse for pain. In his final hours a home care nurse administered some morphine to ease the pain.

By Tuesday night, he was so weak that he could barely talk. When Dr. Gaynor questioned him, he would squeeze his hand in order to reply. He grew restless. He signaled that he wanted to sit up in bed.

His close friend, Fr. Scott Donahue, watched him through the evening. He awoke a few times and signaled again that he wanted to sit up. On Wednesday, President Clinton called. He told Bernardin that both he and Hillary loved him. The call was brief. Bernardin could only utter a whispered "Thank you." They would be his last words.

At 2:30 p.m., John Paul II called. Those at his bedside reported that he seemed to grasp the words, but was unable to reply. Cardinal Roger Mahony had arrived earlier. He informed reporters that they shouldn't read anything into his appearance. "I bought the plane ticket ten days ago," he said. He and Bernardin had forged a friendship in the previous months. The dying cardinal had asked him to preside at his funeral Mass. It meant a great deal to Bernardin, who was terribly hurt by the Eastern cardinals.

At 3:00 p.m., the Los Angeles cardinal said Mass at Bernardin's bedside. He was able to receive the Eucharist. Mahony called the Mass "not one of hopelessness but of hope."

At about 10:00 p.m. we passed the cardinal's residence, and I got out of the car. I wanted to mingle with the media people who had filled the sidewalk outside the home. I counted eleven large TV vans, representing both local and national stations. There must have been two hundred technicians crunched into trucks or behind cameras. It was an electronic death watch that could have offended. Yet, in some peculiar way, the normally aggressive media were remarkably subdued. Only one police officer was on duty and his only responsibility was to insure that a clear path for a single line of cars could provide entrance to Astor Street.

"Isn't this weird?" Mary Ann Ahern of NBC said to me. She had covered the cardinal for years and had come to like him so much that it was difficult for her to contain her feelings. We agreed that it was a strange scene, but that the dying cardinal wouldn't mind.

The church officials appeared to pick up on the social chem-

istry that had been created. In the early days of his administration, it was not unusual to find dozens of police officers,
summoned by some chancery official, guarding the mansion and
keeping the cardinal safe from all harm — and contact. The Bernardin style was evident here even as he lay dying. The respect
he engendered was also present. No one invaded his property.
Throughout the entire death watch and funeral, in fact, only one
two-person camera crew had to be dismissed for overstepping
the unwritten protocols.

Around his second floor bedroom and its adjacent study, two
nuns, Sister Regina and Sister Lucia, his housekeeper and cook,
prayed with Fr. Alvin Zugelter, a retired priest from Cincinnati, who lived in the residence. The cardinal's sister, Elaine, was
there, together with Msgr. Velo and Bishop Goedert and another
friend, Kevin Dowdle, a young, wealthy bond trader, who had
been exceptionally generous to the Catholic schools.

About 4:00 p.m., the cardinal's breathing became labored. The
group took turns by his bed. By 1:00 a.m., the breathing became shallow and Dr. Gaynor told them that the end was near.
Cardinal Mahony started to say the prayers for the dying.

At 1:33 a.m., the breathing stopped.

NINE

"Cardinal, Eminence, You're Home, You're Home"

THE ELEVEN-MEMBER GROUP that had been keeping the vigil gathered in the cardinal's study and comforted each other for about an hour. Then at 2:30 a.m., Bishop Goedert, who would lead the archdiocese until the cardinal's successor was chosen, came to the foot of the steps and announced: "Our brother Joseph is at peace.... As Christians, we believe that Cardinal Bernardin at long last begins a new life, an everlasting life, with our Lord Jesus. We believe that today he will meet his Redeemer face to face.... He was our friend. He was our priest. He was our bishop. But most of all, he was truly our brother Joseph whom he promised to be when he first came into our midst in August 1982. We loved him deeply. We will miss him dearly." Goedert struggled with the brief message. He would nearly break down several times during the days that followed. He was not alone.

By 2:30 a.m. the media had largely withdrawn. Only a few cameras were on hand to record the scene, but it was replayed hundreds of times throughout the day. It was a touching ecclesiastical breakthrough. Bernardin had given the local church permission to cry. In earlier circumstances, Goedert's tearful announcement would have been read as a sign of weakness on his part. When Bernardin's primary physician, Dr. Warren Furey,

shed tears at the press conference announcing the cardinal's cancer sixteen months before and again at the cardinal's funeral, it
was seen as an anomaly. Tears are for aging nuns and house-
hold help. Not for professionals. Furey had become a friend.
Bernardin had given physicians permission to cry, too.

I had left the sidewalk outside the mansion around 11:00 p.m.
By midnight, most of the reporters had gone home, fairly confident that Bernardin would last through the night. Most were
frozen and weary, finding warmth only occasionally wedged into
makeshift seats in the cramped TV trucks.

The announcement unleashed a social and religious epiphany
in Chicago that eclipsed even the funeral of the city's legendary
former mayor, Richard J. Daley, who died in 1976.

✠

The Brother Joseph metaphor may have defined the entire celebration of his life. Like his use of "seamless garment" to cover
and warm the rather clinical "consistent ethic of life," "Brother
Joseph" caught on, cutting through the layers of triumphalist
tradition that only served to separate a church leader from his
people.

The biblical Joseph was the next to the youngest son of Jacob. He had brashly told his brothers of a dream in which he
was made prominent over them. His jealous brothers planned
to murder him, but instead sold him into slavery to a caravan
going to Egypt. They reported to Jacob that Joseph had been
killed. Later, while Joseph languished in prison, the pharaoh was
troubled by bad dreams. When he learned of Joseph's ability to
interpret dreams, he sent for him, and Joseph correctly forecast
seven years of abundant harvest in Egypt, to be followed by
seven years of famine. The pharaoh installed Joseph as his prime
minister, and he wisely raised and stored grain against the seven
years of famine.

When his brothers came to purchase food, they did not recognize him. He revealed himself to them: "I am your brother Joseph, whom you sold into Egypt. And now do not be distressed or angry with yourselves, because you sold me here; for God sent me before you to preserve life" (Gen. 45:4–5). Joseph magnanimously forgave them, moving Jacob and his brothers to Egypt.

The Brother Joseph metaphor helped to define the cardinal's administration. In fact, it may have helped to shape it because it challenged Bernardin to live up to it. In one case, involving a priest who had officiated at an irregular wedding, Bernardin confronted him and said, "Jim, you know I could crush you." He may have felt like doing it. This wasn't Fr. Jim's first rather bizarre pastoral decision, and the cardinal's infinite patience was running low. But he had to live up to his self-declared image and, in this case, the problem was solved by early retirement for the well-meaning but naive priest.

The cardinal used the term first at a ceremony for Chicago priests on the eve of his installation as Chicago's archbishop. In a message that expressed extraordinary hope, he said: "As our lives and ministries are mingled together in the breaking of the bread and the blessing of the cup, I hope that long before my name falls from the eucharistic prayer in the silence of death, you will know well who I am. . . . You will know me as a friend, fellow priest, and bishop. You will know also that I love you. For I am Joseph, your brother!"

The impact of his statement colored his entire term. He was routinely referred to as "Brother Joe." The term itself assuaged anger, even on the lips of those priests who felt they had been wronged or neglected. He also introduced the use of the word "love," a term many clergy found awkward. "I love you," he would frequently say to a priest, even those whom he had to discipline. "Don't make me do this," he urged one priest. "I love you, but you're asking me to do something I can't." The priest withdrew his initiative.

In September, Cardinal Bernardin flew to the Vatican for his final meeting with John Paul II. He was accompanied by Msgr. Kenneth Velo. Somewhere over Greenland, he reached into his briefcase and showed Velo his funeral plans. His associate, who never called him anything but "Cardinal" or "Eminence," began to cry. "Don't worry," Bernardin told him. "I have cried, too."

Not long after the announcement of his death, his body was carried from the mansion. The cameras had hurriedly returned and the mortuary's transferral coffin was carried out the front door by six associates and friends. The mansion has a number of outside doors. Bernardin's Chicago friends could have opted to remove his remains through a side door. But they sensed that he would have none of this. His friend Matt Lamb, a retired funeral director turned artist, guided the pallbearers down the steep steps. He drove the hearse himself in a short procession to one of his local funeral homes where it would remain until the following Monday.

✠

Parish life goes on, even in an archdiocesan cathedral. Holy Name Parish may have upward of six thousand parishioners in a highly transient area. Further, all Catholics within the archdiocese can claim membership in the cathedral parish. It's likely that weddings were scheduled for the weekend and Bernardin would never have permitted his rite of Christian burial to interfere with a celebration. So the opening rites were scheduled for Monday at noon.

The funeral rites would last fifty hours. More than half of the routine hour-long evening newscasts would be devoted to the cardinal's life, details of his death, and his funeral.

My first call came at about 2:30 a.m. A local station with national links asked me to be on their 6:00 a.m. newscast which would be exclusively devoted to the cardinal. In the days that followed, I would receive dozens of calls, as did anyone with any expertise on the cardinal or the workings of the church.

The funeral was exquisitely planned. If Bernardin hadn't planned every detail, those who did understood his mind. Every finely tuned detail revealed his hand and his determination to send messages to his colleagues in the episcopal corps who would flock to his funeral.

On Monday, the procession down State Street from his home to the cathedral was delayed by the final goodbyes of family and friends. His highly polished wooden casket was carried from the mansion by six pallbearers, including his two nephews, a gardener from his home, and two powerful lawyers. A bell choir of students from St. Juliana's and Immaculate Conception parish schools walked along the sidewalk, ringing their multi-pitched bells, while TV cameras recorded the procession and helicopters hovered overhead.

Later, the distant *London Tablet,* a respected Catholic paper, would describe this man as "the most influential American churchman since Martin Luther King, Jr." Somehow, this brief procession reminded one of King's funeral cortege.

The casket was sprinkled with holy water — a remembrance of his baptism. It was covered with a white pall, another reminder of the garment used at baptism and one symbolizing new life. The pall also serves as an equalizer. It is used to cover the coffins of the mighty as well as the homeless who are buried at pauper's funerals. Even American flags, used for funerals of veterans, are removed at the door of the church.

Before the wake service ended, six women — including Bernardin's sister — removed the pall and the coffin was opened. It was another message. Wherever he could, the cardinal encouraged active roles for women in the liturgy. It was also a touching reminder of the women who prepared Christ's body for burial.

Fr. Robert McLaughlin, rector of the cathedral, had returned from a parish tour to China when he learned that the

cardinal had only hours to live. The rector is gifted with a mar-
velous tenor voice, which blended perfectly with the outstanding
cathedral choir and the church's two magnificent organs. "May
Christ, who claimed Joseph in baptism, now enfold him in
his love and bring him to eternal life," McLaughlin told the
congregation, composed mostly of employees of the Pastoral
Center.

I stood across State Street, adding commentary to a local
NBC broadcast. It was bitter cold. The line outside the cathedral, patiently waiting to pay their respects, was only about fifty
people. I recall commenting that, while the mourners would continue to come, it wasn't likely that working people would attempt
to return to downtown Chicago, where parking is always difficult
and the closed-off streets would only exacerbate the problem. I
could not have been more wrong. By 5:00 p.m., the line was
around the block. I went home, largely to catch myself on TV.
By 6:00 p.m., the lines had grown even longer.

Jean and I resolved to return around 11:00 p.m., confident that
we could park in the church lot and enjoy some private moments
with our friend. We could hardly drive by. White-gloved police
just waved us on. The line stretched ten blocks and was estimated
at ten thousand people. By midnight, the crowd had thinned, but
the estimated wait was still ninety minutes.

The Dunkin' Donuts across Chicago Avenue later reported
that their coffee sales were eight times what they usually sold in
the late evenings. The local McDonald's, which carried a sign
reading "Gentle Joseph, Rest in Peace," started distributing coffee free of charge. Later the Red Cross would send a coffee and
sandwich truck.

We went home and returned around 5:00 a.m. the next morning. The line was gone but the church aisle was still filled with
a slow-moving procession of mourners. The cardinal appeared
even thinner than in his final days when his weight had dropped
to 156 pounds and his height had shrunk a remarkable four

inches. He was dressed in white vestments with a white miter. In his hand was a rosary he had used for at least twenty-five years.

✠

Reporters would later describe the event as the largest outpouring since the funeral of John F. Kennedy, a bit of an exaggeration but certainly a phenomenon when measured against the relative importance of both men. The writers in particular wanted to know what brought the people there. Andrew Herrmann, a thoughtful religion writer for the *Chicago Sun-Times*, met a young man who had given up his lunch hour to journey from his loop office. The man told Herrmann about the suicide of a fellow worker's relative and of his visit to that wake service. The cardinal was attending another wake at the same funeral home when he learned of the family's trauma. He came and comforted the family. "I decided a man like that deserved some time from my own life," the man said. "I don't need to eat lunch today."

The coordinator of the funeral rites had ordered a hundred thousand memorial cards, which bore his picture and the famous "Lord, make me an instrument of your peace" prayer of St. Francis. The cards quickly became the hottest relic in town. Long before the wake ended, the supply was exhausted, partly because the crowd was estimated to be a hundred thousand and partly because visitors — especially priests — were seen grabbing fistfuls of them. At least a hundred thousand more were printed and they quickly disappeared. Pastors began to order them for distribution to their congregations. I received two calls from local television stations asking me to appear and "to bring the memorial card."

The wake lasted forty-two hours. Members of the Knights of the Holy Sepulcher and the Knights of Columbus, all dressed in their capes and hats, stood guard over the well-behaved procession. It was something of an irony. Bernardin's relationship with the Knights of Columbus had been a bit strained. They had attended and acted as an honor guard at his installation and Bernardin had remarked after that he felt "uncomfortable" walking under "all those swords." Later, the Knights would abandon their swords and the breach would be healed.

Meanwhile, back at his home, people began placing flowers, pictures, votive candles, cards, and other memorials on the side steps of the mansion, turning it into a shrine. The city sent a squad car to keep an eye on things, but there were no incidents.

Neighborhood mothers brought children. Three tiny girls, partly in awe of all this, responded to their mother's plea to say a prayer. They joined each other in the Grace before Meals.

Throughout the forty-two hours, morning and evening services mixed with several ecumenical services and one for the priests of the archdiocese. A half-dozen choirs sang at the various services. Twelve hundred priests filled the cathedral for a clergy liturgy during which his priests heard a message he had written for them earlier. The text stressed the cardinal's belief that priesthood is a rosary of small acts of concern and thoughtfulness.

"I have never understood what it means to be a priest more than I do now," his letter read. "People look to priests to be authentic witnesses to God's active role in the world, to his love. They don't want us to be politicians or business managers; they are not interested in the petty conflicts that may show up in parish life. Instead, people simply want us to be with them in the joys and sorrows of their lives. No matter how significant our other work might be, the people want something different from their clergy. Even if they are not enamored with or committed to any specific religion, men and women everywhere have a deep desire to come into contact with the transcendent.... The things people remember most are small acts of concern and thoughtfulness. Years later, that is what they tell you about their priest or other clergy."

Bernardin had not always felt that way. In his early years, in common with most bishops, he had given lip service to the apostolate of the "priest in the trenches," but his ministry was generally in an eagle's nest, overseeing the work of others. In the closing years of his life, he came to understand that while a certain amount of organization is important, the priest who "works the curb" after Mass is the one that has an impact.

The homilist was Father Scott Donohue, a close friend of the cardinal. He reminded the priests that the cardinal had "ordained us, anointed us, forgiven, us and challenged us. . . . Simply put, he loved us . . . and told us so each time we gathered."

At the conclusion of the cardinal's message, Fr. Jeremiah Boland said passionately, "Joseph, you were the best." The priests applauded for a full two minutes.

In a letter to his episcopal friend, outspoken and brilliant Bishop William McManus, a native of Chicago and the former bishop of Fort Wayne–South Bend, wrote: "When you chose to call yourself and to be 'Brother Joe,' almost everyone wanted to believe it, and hoped it would be true. Some, however, were skeptical and suspected Chicago quickly would change you from being brother to Boss — Chicago style. . . . Your death has acclaimed you were right."

McManus wanted to avoid the "potted palm" ritual, a clerical term that suggested that bishops said a few meaningless words over the corpse of a deceased office manager who had gotten a good deal on light bulbs for his diocese and kept the lid on the scandal of altar girls.

McManus had clearly differed with the cardinal on many issues. But he could disagree respectfully and Bernardin was never threatened. "Your inspiration," the older bishop wrote, "is my treasure."

✠

Several hundred clergy and laity from fourteen ecumenical religious communities gathered at Holy Name to pay tribute to Brother Joseph. The words of a dying Pueblo Indian elder were read in honor of the Catholic holy man. "When autumn was coming, I went along the path to the mountain," the elder's prayer read. "When it comes time to die, there is rejoicing."

Rev. Stanley Davis, executive director of the National Conference of Christians and Jews, said, "The cardinal's ability to reach out to seemingly everyone with whom he came into contact who was sick or dying was amazing."

"We owe a debt of gratitude to the cardinal, which we must express. For one who does not thank man does not thank God," said Mohammed Kaiseruddin, chairman of the Council of Islamic Organizations of Greater Chicago.

Participants included members of the Native American, Bahai, Buddhist, Hindu, Jain, Muslim, Sikh, Orthodox Christian, and Protestant communities. It reminded one of the cardinal's participation during the summer of 1993 in the Parliament of the World's Religions held in Chicago, where he shared a dais with a spiritual spectrum ranging from Protestant to Buddhists to Wiccans to neo-pagans.

The Jewish service — a first of its kind — began with the prayer "Behold how good and pleasant for brothers to dwell in unity." Although the orthodox and conservative rabbis did not take part, the more liberal rabbis conducted much of the ancient ritual under the dramatic five-hundred-pound wooden crucifix. "He was a jewel from God's crown," said Rabbi Byron Sherwin, vice-president of Spertus Institute of Jewish Studies. "Had there been more people like him during the Holocaust, there would be more people like us, more Jews, alive today."

Three rabbis presided, together with four Jewish community leaders who had accompanied Bernardin on an interfaith trip to the Holy Land. (Before he died, Bernardin was most anxious that advance copies of his book, *A Blessing to Each Other,* would be given to the Jewish leaders. Fr. Thomas Baima, director of Catholic-Jewish Relations for the archdiocese, secured the copies. The book, released in early December, is a compilation of Bernardin's addresses during the historic visit.)

The City Council, normally the battleground for rough and tumble "council wars," held a special session. While the cardinal's family listened — his sister, Elaine, her husband, Jim, their four children, Anna Maria, Jimmy, Joseph, and Angela, cousins from Philadelphia and Columbia and relatives from Italy — Mayor Richard M. Daley said, "He was a full and valued partner in the life of our community."

Meanwhile, the faithful continued to pass by his bier. The numbers must have passed a hundred thousand by noon on November 20.

✠

On the day of the funeral, I went to the press office around 7:00 a.m. to collect a press pass for my boss, Tom Fox, of the *National Catholic Reporter.* Only about a dozen papers were accredited to the cathedral. The remainder had to watch the Rite of Christian Burial on closed circuit television in the adjoining auditorium. Some reporters weren't happy, but the funeral's planners were determined not to turn the event into a tawdry spectacle. It was agreed that the networks would share pool cameras; otherwise the sanctuary would be blocked with cameras and crews.

Since the schedule of rites had been announced, there had been enormous pressure for tickets. The cathedral seats only a little more than twelve hundred and, according to some sources, there were as many as twelve thousand requests.

Earlier, the White House had announced that White House Chief of Staff Leon Panetta would represent the president at the

Mass. But as the interest grew, the president's contingent grew to eleven, including vice-president Al Gore and his wife, Tipper.

The vice-president's presence virtually took control of the funeral out of local hands. More police were assigned, more streets closed off. Trained dogs were led through the cathedral rectory and other buildings, invading priest rooms and sniffing their belongings. Each priest was instructed on precisely how their window blinds were to be arranged. The deceased cardinal would have been bemused by all this.

One elderly priest, Msgr. John J. Egan, who had celebrated his eightieth birthday just a few weeks before, had a brief dizzy episode just as the procession was to begin. Vice-president Gore, who had entered through the rectory, assigned his Irish Catholic physician to attend him.

Leon Panetta did come, together with Secretary of Health and Human Services Donna Shalala and Secretary of Housing and Urban Development Henry Cisneros. There were several high-level White House assistants, together with the ambassador to the Vatican, Raymond Flynn, and the director of the Peace Corps, Mark Gearan. For those who measure such things, it was a delegation worthy of a head of state. Illinois Governor Jim Edgar shared a pew with Mayor Richard M. Daley.

The carefully calibrated procession of dignitaries was led by ecumenical leaders of all faiths. They were followed by hundreds of diocesan and religious priests, 157 visiting bishops and archbishops, and 9 American cardinals, 2 of them from the Vatican. Eleven clerical masters of ceremonies were required to herd the shepherds and ranking sheep into preassigned places.

Cardinal Roger Mahony, archbishop of Los Angeles, presided at the exquisitely planned liturgy—one that bore the clear prints of Cardinal Bernardin. Mahony had known the cardinal since their days at Catholic University of America and their years as leaders of the NCCB. He shared much of Bernardin's interest in minorities and was one of the backers of Bernardin's Com-

mon Ground Project. It's likely that the Los Angeles cardinal
was Bernardin's closest friend among the American cardinals.

Following Cardinal Mahony's greeting, Cardinal William
Baum, former archbishop of Washington and now prefect of the
curia's Major Penitentiary, who acted as John Paul II's personal
representative, together with Archbishop Agostino Cacciavillan, pro-nuncio to the United States, brought the Holy Father's
personal blessings and gratitude.

It was standard stuff. The message traced Bernardin's career
and expressed hope of resurrection. But in the weeks that followed, rumors from the Vatican suggested that John Paul II
genuinely viewed Bernardin as a pastoral man and appeared to
understand that his successor must continue in that spirit.

Msgr. Kenneth Velo delivered a witty, insightful homily, mer
cifully devoid of cliches. It was sprinkled with humor that
brought laughter and applause from a congregation of clerical
and lay leaders and warmth to the hundreds standing outside the
cathedral on a portion of State Street which had just been named
in honor of the cardinal.

"God has touched you through the life of Cardinal Bernardin," he said. "Didn't he teach us? Didn't he show us the way?"
Velo asked rhetorically, while the congregation applauded. It
was a magnificently constructed homily that brought laughter
and tears.

"He had a hard time with people who directed lives by using rear-view mirrors," Velo said. "He wanted people to come
around the table and to see not what divides us, but what brings
us together. He wanted to make common ground, holy ground.
Leaders of the church, pick up the torch of Jesus, of John XXIII,
of Joseph Bernardin, that all may be one." (People noted afterward that John XXIII was the only pope mentioned. Chances
are, this meant nothing in particular, but it reflected the mood
of the people.)

It seemed clear that the young monsignor was telegraphing

messages to the bishops. Most followed his homily with energy. They joined in the laughter and the applause. But the front row of cardinals and senior archbishops barely responded. They sat, stone-faced, their hands on their knees. They appeared unaccustomed to a spontaneous liturgical celebration.

There was a moment of silence following the homily. Then the entire cathedral burst into thunderous applause and rose to its feet — a message as powerful as the homily itself. At least two television stations rebroadcast the entire homily and the print media carried lengthy portions of it. The Pastoral Center and the *Chicago Tribune*, which promised copies of the homily, was inundated with calls. I called Tom Fox at the *National Catholic Reporter*. He had tried repeatedly to pick up the homily on the Internet. But the lines were jammed.

✠

Following the two-hour Mass, a hundred-car cortege, followed by at least a dozen buses, made its way to Mount Carmel Cemetery through streets selected by the late cardinal. He wanted to pass through neighborhoods that reflected the diversity of his archdiocese. Along the route, students and employees of church-related institutions gathered outside to pay their respects. It took nearly two hours to cover the seventeen miles to the door of the Bishops' Mausoleum, where hundreds waited in light but wind-driven snow.

In the weeks that followed, crowds continued to visit the Bishops' Mausoleum. A report on December 8 said that more than forty thousand had come and that the eighteen-crypt tomb would remain open to accommodate the crowds. The officials at Mount Carmel even set up a Bishops' Mausoleum Information Telephone Line. I called a dozen times, only to get a busy signal.

Bernardin, who rarely missed a funeral of one of his priests, had a signature commendation which was recalled by Bishop

Timothy Lyne, retired auxiliary and vicar for senior priests. "We commend him to the God he loved so much," he would say, "to the God he served so well." Lyne applied it to Bernardin.

Bishop Raymond Goedert, vicar general of the archdiocese, choked as he delivered the final farewell. Again, he was not alone. Cardinal Mahony, the presider, was heard to say that he had never witnessed such an outpouring of feeling since the death of John XXIII.

✠

In the weeks that followed, while the news turned to other things, including endless speculation on Bernardin's successor, the cardinal's name was rarely far from the front pages. There were stories of favors received. The Internet developed a virtual scrapbook, filled with remembrances. WGN-TV offered the entire five-hour liturgy on two VCR tapes with the proceeds going to the Little Sisters of the Poor, who had been caring for the cardinal's mother ever since he arrived in Chicago. He had asked people that, in lieu of flowers, they should make contributions to the congregation. The sisters were reluctant to reveal the amount received but suggested that the gifts were plentiful.

The staid *Chicago Tribune* ran a lengthy piece about possible canonization. They quoted a visitor to the tomb who said, "If they do make him a saint, they should make him the patron of reconciliation." Successful or not, there is more than a good chance that, after a decent interval — five years seems to be the norm — some people will organize to persuade the new archbishop to set up a tribunal to examine his life and writings with a view to naming him a servant of God, the first step in the ladder to the canon of the saints. Already intuitively cautious, an official at the Pastoral Center would say, "Only time will tell."

✠

At the opening of his homily, Msgr. Velo had introduced himself as "the regular driver," a term applied to him by Bernardin's aged mother. Often, toward the end of their many journeys through the city, Velo would say to the snoozing cardinal: "Cardinal, we're here. We've arrived." As his homily drew to a close, Msgr. Velo said, "But I ask you to allow me just a few words with the cardinal. You see, it has been a long, long and beautiful ride.

"Cardinal, Eminence," he said. "You're home. You're home."